PLEASE DON'T BITE THE BABY
(and Please Don't Chase the Dogs)

Please Don't Bite the Baby

(And Please Don't Chase the Dogs)

keeping our kids and our dogs
safe and happy together

LISA J. EDWARDS

SEAL PRESS

Seal Press
A Member of the Perseus Books Group
1700 Fourth Street
Berkeley, California
sealpress.com

Library of Congress Cataloging-in-Publication Data is available.

ISBN: 978-1-58005-577-2

10 9 8 7 6 5 4 3 2 1

Cover and interior design by Domini Dragoone
Author photo with Indy and Pinball by Jill Ferson
Printed in the United States of America
Distributed by Publishers Group West

Please Don't Bite the Baby *is dedicated to all the parents who love their children and love their not-quite-so-perfect dogs, to all the dogs who have lost their homes or lives because they didn't know what to do with their new tiny family member, and to all the children whose family has a dog.*

Contents

Preface

....

We love our dogs. They are family and they love us unconditionally. We believe they will love our children, too, and
they usually do. However, this love is not always enough to prevent the more than 4.5 million dog bites the Centers for Disease
Control (CDC) estimates occur annually in the United States—
that equals a dog bite every seven seconds. According to the
American Veterinary Medical Association, every forty seconds
someone seeks medical attention for a dog bite–related injury,
and 70 percent of the total dog bites annually (3.15 million) injure
children under the age of fifteen.

In contrast, the number of swimming-related injuries for
children under fourteen is just under four thousand per year.
When I compare the four thousand annual swimming-related
injuries to the over three million dog bite–related injuries, I
am left scratching my head. I wonder why people tell me they
don't worry about leaving their dog alone with their kids, but
those same people would never dream of letting their children
swim alone.

People assume their good dog and their children will be fine together. Not only do the statistics tell us to be more careful, the tragic experiences of too many individuals speak to the necessity for more vigilance. As you read this book and apply the basic tips I have outlined, you will help keep your baby safe from your dog, and your dog safe from your baby so your children can grow up with their whole family—two- and four-legged—and look back with love and affection on their first doggie love.

JILL FERSON

Lisa, Indy, and Pinball

CHAPTER ONE

The Ruff Wait
for a Baby

Before I had any notion I would have a baby in my life, I frequently worked with clients whose dogs' behavioral problems fell into the dog-baby or dog-toddler category. I remember one smart Schipperke in particular. She was the only dog who ever figured out how to unzip my treat bag—a red flag. She was too smart, enthusiastic, and driven.

I asked the parents if anything had changed in her life when the baby arrived. They said no and then outlined the dog's issues: "She jumps up on the kitchen chairs and begs for food at the table. She growls and bites at us when we push her off. She won't get off the bed, and she barks and growls at the baby when he's playing."

I asked a little more and they said, "We always used to let her sit on the chairs and feed her at the table . . . then the baby came, and we stopped that." Clearly, they didn't realize they had actually changed a lot.

I watched how their son played around the dog. Pushing a toy lawn mower that made a scary noise, he chased the ten-pound dog around the apartment while Mom and Dad laughed, until the Schipperke turned on the menacing lawn mower and growled. Then they yelled at the dog.

This dog's life had been turned upside-down when the baby appeared and went from bad, when so many things in her life had changed, to scary, when the little boy was allowed to frighten her daily. It's hard to tell parents that their baby is tormenting their dog, and it is even harder to help people realize and accept that they and their child have contributed to their dog's dangerous behavior. I struggled to convince these parents that allowing their son to do whatever he wanted to with this dog was dangerous. In the end, management, training, and guidance allowed them to keep the little dog they loved with them through a second child and beyond.

Without the realization that we as parents have to protect our dogs from our babies in order to protect our babies from our dogs, we may find ourselves facing one of the worst choices in our lives—between the safety of our baby and the life of our dog.

With a bit of mindfulness and preparation, most of us can avoid ever having to make this choice.

FOR THE FIRST TEN YEARS of our marriage, my husband, Lawrence, was opposed to having children. We both knew the statistics regarding abuse passing from one generation to the next, and unfortunately both of us experienced childhood abuse, which I detailed in *A Dog Named Boo: The Underdog with a Heart of Gold*. I was hopeful that years of learning to understand our upbringings, along with our slightly oddball sense of humor, would allow us to break the cycle, but Lawrence was not convinced. "It would be when it would be" was my refrain and, meanwhile, my dogs offered me an outlet for my mothering instincts.

Atticus, my first dog, was there for me before my husband entered the picture—in fact, Atticus introduced me to Lawrence.

The first words I said to Lawrence were, "What are you doing to my dog?" I walked in on him trying to engage Atticus in a chase game with the Baby Dino-Roar—one of the many dog toys scattered around the office. Atticus was happily complying, which meant Lawrence was on Atticus's approved list.

I will always be grateful to Atticus for introducing me to my husband and for bringing me through some of the darker times of my life as I processed my past. I learned lessons from that devoted dog I never learned from my human family—how to love unconditionally and without being violated. After finding me my husband, Atticus seemed to conspire with Lawrence to find Dante at a dog run in the East Village. Not usually a big player at dog parks, Atticus was actively playing with the emaciated yet gregarious and joyful Dante. Between bouts of play, Atticus would return to my spot on the bench as if to check in and Dante would follow him. At each of these check-ins Atticus, Dante, and Lawrence would all employ their big begging eyes in support of Lawrence's case for bringing Dante home with us. A few years later, I found Boo when I stumbled upon his litter one fateful Halloween. They had been dumped outside a pet store that could best be compared to the shop from the Stephen King novel, *Needful Things*. This pet store, like Stephen King's store, disappeared without a trace a month after I found Boo.

These three dogs walked me through a learning and growth process in a way that demands my eternal gratitude. After Atticus pulled me out of a deep, dark hole and taught me how to love, Dante taught me how to be joyful and guided me toward a newfound confidence. Boo was able to heal the last of my old wounds as he worked his magic, not only on Lawrence and me, but also on the thousands of strangers he visited during the years he worked with me as a therapy dog.

Boo's patience and gentleness with children allowed me to take him to visit kids in schools, libraries, and hospitals. In addition, he visited adults with developmental disabilities and seniors in nursing homes. Our work with kids simultaneously soothed my need for my own child while highlighting the emptiness I felt.

While Boo and I were visiting children, Lawrence was percolating on the subject of kids. Boo had cerebellar hypoplasia, a neurological condition that caused him difficulty in walking and learning and affected his vision. At first, these needs pushed Lawrence's buttons. But as he began to accept Boo and learn to be patient, Lawrence realized that he was not the same as his biological father had been and maybe, given the chance, he could be a very different parent. Lawrence has a singular approach to change, best illustrated by the now semi-legendary dishwasher episode.

"We don't need a dishwasher," he said. "I'm a dishwasher."

I made my case, failed to convince him, and installed the dishwasher anyway. Within a month, Lawrence said, "I love this dishwasher!"

While I was used to this approach for mundane matters, I never expected him to wake up one morning and tell me out of the blue, "We should have a child."

By the time he did, Atticus was gone and his successor, Porthos, was already four years old. Boo had been visiting with different schoolchildren and seniors and doing library reading visits for almost six years. My dog-training business was doing well. Dante was slowing down with age, and a cat we later named Freya had literally fallen out of a tree and moved in with us. Our animals had taught us we could parent with love and patience, but our bodies were not cooperating as we struggled to become pregnant. Lawrence and I were wildly unsuccessful at producing a child on our own, even with intrauterine insemination (IUI) or in vitro fertilization (IVF) using donor eggs. After our last IVF ended in miscarriage, we realized it was time to adopt a child who needed us as much as we wanted him or her.

On some levels, the process of adopting a child was easier than infertility treatments: no daily shots, no blood tests. I could have coffee and chocolate along with a glass of wine with dinner and have no guilt over having too much stress in my life. On other levels, it was also much harder: we were expected to put ourselves into a fifteen- to twenty-page catalogue (the *profile*) with pictures of us, our family, and our home, along with exciting descriptions, to entice a birth mother or parents to pick us over the thousands of other couples wishing to start a family. The process was like waiting to hear your name called for a game of elementary school kickball—only this was the most important game of our lives.

As uncomfortable and challenging as it was to advertise ourselves, it became even more difficult when the adoption case-worker demanded I eliminate everything about the dogs from our profile except a brief paragraph.

"It shouldn't be so much about the dogs," she said.

I wanted to explain that my life *was* all about dogs, and if we had to sell ourselves like a time-share I needed to be comfortable with what we included. Instead I just said, "I work with dogs, I volunteer with dogs, and we have dogs. They need to be repre-sented in the profile."

Throwing in the towel, she replied, "Of course, it's your pro-file and you can do what you like. We just know dogs are not a *selling* point."

These dogs were my children when I had none and they were there to comfort me through various challenges in my life. They had been the greatest teachers I had ever had. I was a full-time dog trainer and behavioral consultant: dogs were my work and our primary source of income, and the volunteer animal-assisted therapy I did with them was my passion. The dogs were going to be a part of our child's life, and it was important for the birth parents to love dogs as much as I did, especially if a love of dogs had any genetic component. It was also critical for the birth parents to understand the extent to which our child would be exposed to dogs, in case of a genetic predisposition to allergies. Our child would truly be enveloped in dogs from the very beginning. With my usual damn-the-torpedoes approach, I included the dogs in the profile—*on several pages*.

The adoption agency indicated that the normal wait time to be chosen was anywhere from three months to three years. With many of the staff reiterating that dogs should not be in the profile because it would turn off birth parents and they would look to another couple, who knew how much longer it would take for us with the inclusion of the dogs in our profile? The wide time frame made it hard to gauge when to begin training my dogs for a baby. Ideally, training the dog should begin as soon as a woman finds out she is pregnant—allowing about eight months to proof the initial skills and to begin desensitizing the dog to some of the stranger baby gizmos like newborn car seats that may be carried at the dog's eye level, toys that beep or sing, automated swings that seem to move on their own, and crying sounds coming from a baby monitor. We know it is just the sound of the baby amplified from another room, but what does the dog think? It is usually a good idea to pair these items with fun games, meals, or treats so they learn to love—not fear—these items. I didn't worry about Dante and Boo with baby gadgets—they had both seen so many different items on therapy visits that they were pretty solid. However, Porthos could be an anxious dog, so I wanted to do some work with him on these toys and contraptions.

It was also time for me to assess my dogs' basic commands, including *sit, down, stay, wait, settle,* and *come.* Dante and Porthos were dead-on in terms of their general commands and the all-important *settles*, while Boo was average. His love of kids made up for it and with age his *settles* were becoming much better.

Even though my dogs had good basic skills, there is always room to improve before a baby comes home. With the caseworker's words—"Dogs are just not a selling point"—repeating in my head, I had very little faith that any birth parents would pick us. Because of the nagging feeling that it would be a long wait, I couldn't bring myself to start the proofing or desensitizing for the baby thingamajigs. Instead, I worked skills at a distance so I could give the dogs commands from across the room or from another room, and I reminded them of their group commands so I could give them cues like, "All dogs, *sit*" or "All dogs, *down*." This prevents doggie Whac-A-Mole, in which one dog complies when he hears his name and the others break, thinking they are done (and around it goes!). In a household without a baby, doggie Whac-A-Mole is annoying, but with a baby in the home it becomes potentially dangerous and tiresome for already exhausted parents. I reminded myself that all three of my dogs had passed their Pet Partners therapy dog evaluations—they were pretty good dogs. But, as in so many cases, too much knowledge isn't always a comfort. I knew from years as a dog trainer that dogs don't generalize well. I could not assume that because they were good on visits, they would be okay with automatic baby paraphernalia, or a real live crying baby in their home. Many good dogs have made horrible mistakes with children.

At the beginning of the first year of our wait, Dante let us know his time had come. At thirteen years old, and after two strokes and a cancer diagnosis, he needed to rest. We let him go with the help of my friend Julie, who euthanized him in his favorite spot in our backyard while other friends came to support us.

Just before he passed away, I asked him to come back next time as something a bit smaller. I said, "Maybe Beagle-sized."

Later that day, I was certain Dante sent me a sign when, after cleaning vegetables, I went out to discard the scraps in the woods for the critters. There, about six feet from where I was standing, was a brown bear—looking at me. I said, "Hello there," and he looked at me as if thinking for a second and then casually romped off into the woods. Dante's markings had always resembled a Kodiak bear's, and there was no question in my mind that this was *his* farewell. I wanted to believe it meant he'd be back.

Two months later, a pregnant dog came into the shelter where I consult. I didn't think much about it until I looked at her eyes and saw her eyeliner—identical to Dante's. The shelter president told me that apparently the mama-dog had been tied up in her yard when a roving Beagle took an interest and, voila, the pups were on their way. Dante was a very literal dog and, since Boo, I have been driven by signs and portents when choosing my dogs.

I was at the shelter the day this mama-dog gave birth to seven of the cutest puppies—six girls and one boy. I was overjoyed at the prospect of having a girl-dog for once. Lawrence, Boo, and Porthos all picked the fluffy little girl-dog we named Callie when I was fostering all seven puppies at home during the holidays. As this was the first litter I had raised from birth in the shelter and fostered at home, I was devastated when they came down with parvovirus (a highly contagious deadly disease). The boy-dog responded to home treatment, but the girls were all admitted to intensive care. After ten days, we were able to bring our fluffy, tiny Callie home. A week later she had a massive seizure and died in my arms on the way to the emergency vet.

Lawrence and I were averaging a death every six months—first my miscarriage, then Dante, and then Callie. We needed to break the pattern, and all Lawrence could say was, "We have to take Pinball."

Pinball was the only puppy from that litter not adopted—the only boy. I reminded Lawrence that Pinball was trouble. He was an extremely high-energy, seemingly jet-fueled, pushy puppy who lacked confidence but played hard, jumped high, and howled like a Beagle. Neither Porthos nor Boo was keen on him. Was this Dante? Was there a reason Pinball was destined for us? The answers to these questions didn't matter. We were both too emotional to do anything other than adopt Pinball—we needed some joy.

If all the Impressionist painters got together and created the quintessential image of a dog, it would be Pinball. With his long flowing fringe that billows in the breeze, floppy orange ears, and big-eyed innocent face, he exuded *cute*. Social with dogs and people, he was extremely quick to learn commands and very willing to try new things. But as he matured, his fears began to surface and his resource guarding (fiercely guarding objects), which started early, was off the charts. He bit Lawrence (no puncture) when he was only four months old over the squeaker from a toy. We were well into the adoption process at this point, but no baby was on the horizon. I worked with Pinball, hoping to win the race between fixing his behavior and introducing a baby into the household.

Pinball went to classes with me and eagerly learned tricks, and his resource guarding was improving. But he was young and still had a few developmental periods to go through. Dogs, like children, have pretty well established developmental milestones. Just as children have their terrible twos and adolescence, dogs have five stages that typically come with increased fears and the potential social anxiety or avoidance that goes with them. I would have to work hard with Pinball to be sure these fear-periods didn't result in an adult fear-aggressive dog who was also a resource guarder. It was going to take a lot of management and oversight, along with training, to keep a baby safe while keeping the dogs we loved.

We had put up gates so I could allow Pinball and Porthos to safely adjust to each other and I could begin some of the baby prep work like training them to obey commands over gates, at a distance, and from other rooms, as well as go-to-place commands to easily send the dogs to a specific spot. Because the gates were see-through, the dogs could be apart but not totally isolated, and I could work multiple dogs simultaneously (on either side of the gates) to build positive associations and good relationships between them as they worked, played, and were rewarded together. I would use the same technique once baby arrived, except I would be with the baby on one side of the gate while I gave commands and rewards to the dogs on the other side of the gate. This would allow the dogs to work around the baby safely, letting them get to know him or her up close but with boundaries.

At the end of the first year of our wait, it was time for our second annual home study. In that meeting, the social worker asked if we were frustrated by the wait and seemed to brace herself for the response she expected. I told her the wait was much like the day Dallas ran off with me. Dallas was a colossal horse who apparently needed a break from the group ride we were on and the fact that I was on his back was no more a hindrance to him than the flies around his ears. Without warning, his body jerked and I launched. I pulled back on the behemoth's reins to no effect, except that I think his horsey ears flipped me off. I could do nothing but try to stay on him. I believed he would stop at some point; then I could figure out the next step—get off, call for help, and so on.

I had never galloped before, so staying on was a struggle. I clenched my legs around his girth, and locked my hands on the saddle. Eventually Dallas did stop and I heard hoof beats behind me as Cowboy Bob arrived with a laugh and said, "That was pretty good. Most folks would have fallen off a quarter mile ago."

I had only enough air for a short reply, and said, "Falling was not an option."

The process of waiting for a birth mother or parents to pick us was like staying on Dallas—it was the only option. The lesson that horse taught me that day was a powerful gift that allowed me to live through our adoption wait without the aggravation that often accompanies it.

Still afraid that if I began desensitizing the dogs to baby thingamajigs I would jinx everything, I focused instead on my business—teaching dog-training classes and meeting with clients. I wrote a memoir about the therapy work Boo and I did together in *A Dog Named Boo*. I taught Pinball to *settle* under my desk as I typed. I redesigned Lawrence's office, creating a custom hand-made wall unit that had cubbies and drawers for great storage as a nursery or an upgraded study, depending on how things went. Because my tools were limited, I joked with friends that it was like catering a wedding with an Easy-Bake Oven. The complications of this project kept me focused on what I could control, while my doubts about the outcome of our adoption quest were intensified by the agency's statement that we would probably parent an "instant baby." This is a situation in which a birth mother delivers a baby without an adoption plan in place. When the agency is called, they call the next adoptive couple in line—usually well after a couple has exhausted the three-year wait. An instant baby usually leaves the adoptive parents with one or two days' notice to get to the hospital and pick up their child. The anxiety of possibly having to leave at a moment's notice was compounded by all the moving pieces of our life. Who would drop everything to come take care of our dogs if we had to leave in a moment's notice? Who would give Porthos his insulin injections twice a day? Who would handle the nutty Pinball or gently steer Boo through the outside door, up and down the stairs off the deck to the yard, and up and down the thirteen steps to our bedroom where he slept at night?

At the beginning of year two, we had what the agency calls a fall-through, in which a birth mother or birth parents begin the adoption process but change their minds, deciding either to parent or choose another couple. In our case they chose to parent. This process, which the agency acknowledged would include at least one or two fall-throughs for each adoptive couple, seemed designed to diminish hope; so at the end of year two when we received an email stating that another couple was interested in our profile, we were very cautious. We had three months to be completely ready for a baby, or not. This was not the instant baby the agency had predicted. Somebody out there *did* like us!

Uncertainty, anxiety, and guarded hope permeated everything. Lawrence and I had multiple debates: Do we cancel our vacation? Who will take care of all the dogs —not just for a couple of days, but potentially three weeks or more? What do I tell my students when I have to cancel classes for an unspecified period of time? Do we prepare at all given the fact that the birth mother would have seven days after we had custody of the baby in which to change her mind? Do we buy baby paraphernalia yet?

We bought a car seat. Everything else could wait.

Those three months were the longest and shortest months of our lives. We spoke at length to the birth parents and cashed in all our miles to fly down to meet them for lunch so they could get a sense of us and be sure we were the right couple for their adoption plan. We came to know and like them—and, in an ironic twist, it was the home with pets to which they were drawn because we cherished animals as much as they did. I chuckled as I remembered the caseworker's words: it turned out it *was* all about the dogs.

Just when I was hopeful, the caseworker called to say that

a relative of the birth mother was worried about the dogs and the baby. She had asked the caseworker, "Will her dogs accept the baby?"

There had been two horrible news items about babies who had been fatally attacked by dogs, one not too far from where the inquiring relative lived.

All I could say was, "It's never about if the dogs will be okay—that thinking leads to trouble. The real question should be, 'Are the parents prepared to introduce the dogs and the baby slowly and happily, and are they prepared to manage the dogs around the baby to maintain safety?'"

I knew that answer, while correct, was not what the relative was looking for—and that this conversation could potentially mark the end of the adoption plan.

Was she right to ask? I couldn't even count the number of calls and emails I received from frazzled parents (or grandparents) that read almost exactly the same way: "My son or daughter just brought home their first baby. Their ten-year-old dog acted aggressively toward the baby, but no harm done. Can they avoid having to get rid of the dog?" Or, "Our daughter has just started toddling and our dog growled at her yesterday. Can we keep the dog?" Some of the clients I heard from chose to try to work things out. But many gave up and found a shelter or rescue, re-homed the dog with friends or relatives, or euthanized the dog.

Often folks will say, "It's easy for you—you're a *trainer!*"

The reality is that my being a behavioral professional may actually make things harder. My understanding of dog behaviors and triggers makes it illogical for me to penalize them for any mistakes they make because of fear, anxiety, or things we humans may have done to aggravate the situation. And no matter how good a trainer I might be, I was faced with a houseful of complicated dogs. This leveled the playing field: a home with one easygoing dog plus a novice handler was equal to my home with three complicated dogs and one cat plus a professional—or some kind of similar math. It was not going to be any easier for me just because I was a trainer.

Boo, at fourteen, affectionate yet often confused and almost completely blind, could be a hazard to himself and others as he felt his way around the house, bumping into everyone and everything.

Porthos—smart, friendly, but sometimes suspicious of men—had injured every other pet who lived in our house. Would he make the distinction between a human baby and another pet? What do dogs think of human babies? Making an amazing observation, Lawrence once said, "I bet to the dogs we seem immortal. It probably looks like we don't age at all while they go through their whole lifetimes, from puppies to old dogs, with us changing very little in that time."

Dogs who watch children grow up may have a better sense of the human process and most dogs probably figure it out, but I cannot say with certainty that dogs understand what a human baby is right away. Human babies don't walk, talk, or even smell like adults, and from a dog's perspective they probably don't look anything like adults. It's hard to believe that a dog will look at the human baby and say, "That's a little person. He looks nothing like a big person—he can't even touch the top of his head—but yep, that's a little person. . . ."

I hoped that Porthos would not see the new baby as another pet. And even if he did understand the concept of a baby, we also had to contend with his medical and psychological issues that triggered his worst behaviors. Both Porthos's diabetes and severe obsessive-compulsive disorder (OCD) came with mood swings and anxiety that could start a cascade of behaviors that sometimes resulted in redirected aggression. As a result, Porthos required a high level of daily oversight.

Then there was Pinball: While sensitive and affectionate, he was the real accident waiting to happen. Pinball gave very little warning when he was feeling distressed—no growl, just a hard stare over a resource (that could easily be missed)—and has shown a willingness to bite.

When clients tell me their dog has growled at their child and I say, "Good," they look at me as if I'm nuts. Growling is a dog's fire alarm. The dog who growls allows you to get everyone safe and managed in times of trouble. The dog who does not growl is like a busted fire alarm.

I had to muster the courage to look at my dogs dispassionately and ask what I could do to keep a baby safe around each of them. First, the dogs needed to learn to make the right choices around a baby. Second, I needed to have more ways to physically manage the dogs so I could separate them from the baby at any given time to keep the baby safe in case of mistakes while we were all learning. I realized I needed more preplanned strategies that incorporated the dogs' trained skills and physical management for a house that would be brimming with the chaos of three dogs, the instigating cat who often set the dogs off, and a newborn. I had a fence we couldn't afford put in around the backyard, knowing there would be times I'd need to let the dogs outside without oversight, and I added a couple of more gates to other doorways so each dog could be gated in a separate part of the house if need be.

As we got closer to the due date, our friends and family were on standby to take care of our brood while we spent an open-ended amount of time away, waiting for travel clearances from each state. Because adoptions take months (at best) to finalize, parents in the adoptive process have to get permission to both leave and enter a state with a child in custody. There was no predicting how long we would be gone—three or four days if the birth parents changed their minds or a month if state clearances took longer than we hoped.

Lawrence's parents stayed at our house with Boo, Pinball, and Freya-the-cat, giving us daily updates via Facebook and email. The new fence made their job easier and it went pretty well, save for one day when they spent hours afraid they'd lost Pinball until he emerged with a stretch from his hidey-hole under the ottoman. This was a reminder of the things that could easily set the Rube Goldberg–esque canine chaos contraption into motion.

Porthos stayed separately in my friend Kim's basement guest apartment, where she slept each night (to her husband's chagrin) to be sure Porthos didn't have a seizure or an OCD episode. Her job was tougher than the others', given the daily collection of urine for testing and insulin injections to regulate his diabetes.

A week into our wait in North Carolina, our son's birth father entered the maternity ward waiting room and announced, "It's a boy. Follow me." The complications of my son's birth rival the canine complications of his new home and will one day be a story he can tell when he is ready.

Meanwhile, maintaining the pet care while we were gone was like balancing eggs on the tip of a pin from five hundred miles away and waiting for it to come crashing down in a big *splat*. Two weeks into our wait in North Carolina, Lawrence's parents had to leave and shortly after that, Porthos got booted out of Kim's comfy apartment to make room for another dog with a prior reservation. Luckily, friends of mine volunteered to take turns staying at the house or dropping by to look after the animals. It was as if every day we remained in the hotel with a newborn, waiting for clearance to leave the state, I could hear a dramatic soundtrack building in the background. On the one hand, I was worried about the animals, and on the other hand, we had to spend the first ten days of our son's life in a hotel room doing all the things that newborns are not supposed to do.

The pediatrician, who saw us before we could leave, told us, "You guys are in a very unique position and you have to be able to buy food, supplies, eat a hot meal, and just get out so you don't go mad. He's gonna have to go with you—just be cautious."

This made for some early parenting doubts as we brought our three-day-old son to the buffet breakfast (the weather was good so we could eat outside to minimize his exposure to germs), took him to the grocery store and baby store for supplies, and even went out to restaurants. Eating dinner at four in the afternoon usually guaranteed an empty restaurant and less exposure for the baby. However, one evening a family came in as we were finishing and their little boy was fascinated with our tiny companion. The mother asked, "How old is he?"

When I said, "Six days," she made an audible gasp and gave me a stabbing glare before she forcibly turned her son around.

I avoided conversations like this for the rest of our stay.

Nineteen days after we left New York, we finally received clearance to leave North Carolina with our newborn son, Indigo. On our two-day drive home (stopping every two hours to change poopy diapers), I went over and over in my head how I wanted the dogs to greet us, and how I wanted them to meet Indy. It was essential that they got to greet us happily and normally and that their first meeting with the baby was positive.

I texted my housesitting friends Bonnie, Jill, and Linda with my strategy. The plan was simple—I would hand Indy to his aunties at the door and the dogs would get me all to themselves so Lawrence could unpack our car, which looked like a getaway car from a baby store heist. With this plan, the control of chaos had begun.

Training Tips You Can Try at Home

★ Assessing your dog's skills
★ Desensitization and Counter-Conditioning (DS/CC)
★ Proofing behaviors

★ **Your dog's skills** should be based on your household's needs. Not every dog in every home needs to obey the same reliable commands. The more dogs and/or the more kids you have, the more skills your dogs will need.

The Canine Good Citizen (CGC) test, as part of the American Kennel Club's CGC Program, is an excellent basic test of a dog's skills and was designed to lay the foundation for further training and activities. The CGC test is a snapshot of your dog's performance in a formal setting while you give your undivided attention to your dog. It cannot, however, measure your dog in your household with your new baby or tell you how he will react when your home is brimming with guests visiting your baby. It also doesn't test for resource guarding, off-leash distance skills, or your dog's comfort on the other side of gates or in a crate. When assessing a dog to see if his skills are going to be sufficient for the upcoming or newly arrived baby, the CGC test is a great measurement of basic skills and you need to review those skills in the context of your daily routine with your dog and your new (or anticipated) routine with your baby, and then overlay the physical makeup of your home so you can assess where you will need which skills. Your dog will need the following basic skills: *sit, down, off, wait, drop it, leave it, loose-leash walking,* and the most important of all— *SETTLE.* (More details on these later.)

☆ Your dog should ideally be able to perform the above skills after one verbal command, nine times out of ten, off leash, in any room of the house, with you in any position (standing, sitting, lying down—it matters), and with only an intermittent occasional reward.

☆ If you are regularly repeating any command several times and/or increasing your tone of voice to get your dog to comply, then your dog does not have reliable behaviors and it is time to return to consistent rewards for all your dog's good behaviors. It is important to let go of what the dog *should do* and focus on what the dog does do in order to improve his skills to the desired level.

☆ Over time, as your dog becomes more reliable, you will be able to move to an intermittent reward schedule.

☆ Remember, the only way to completely fade out the treat is to be sure your *praise* always precedes the treat! (See "Proofing Behaviors" below.) In the end you will have correction-free and hands-free commands.

☆ If you have determined that you need to return to consistent reinforcement (by rewarding) for training new or improving longstanding skills, your dog will be very happy that baby arrived and began this "new" trend in treating. And you will get a twofer—a dog who is happy about the baby's arrival and the ability to control the dog with verbal commands to keep the baby safe.

★ **Desensitization and counter-conditioning (DS/CC)**
refer to making the dog less sensitive around a trigger (desensitization), while also changing her associations and emotions to be more positive about the trigger (counter-conditioning).

TRAINING TIPS

The trigger can be anything a dog is unfamiliar with, afraid of, or really excited by. It is not enough for your dog to just see a trigger or be around a trigger to desensitize her. You have to be careful to expose her to the trigger only at the point at which she can tolerate it without reacting—this is called subthreshold. This type of exposure will desensitize her over time. But that may not be enough either if she is already afraid of the trigger—then we have to change her emotions, too, by pairing the subthreshold exposure with a primary reinforcer that is of high enough value that she and her brain are totally wowed. For some dogs a super-high-value primary reinforcer could be cheese, for others a tennis ball. But it can be anything and everything in between as well. Your dog has to tell you what her most valuable primary reinforcer is—and generally your praise will not be enough, though it should definitely be in the mix.

If you are matching the presentation of the primary reinforcer effectively with the trigger, soon your dog will be consciously looking forward to the trigger. Then later, through neuroplasticity, her brain will physically change the signals it sends along her neural pathways when the trigger appears. Instead of her "That scares me," signal, her neurons will be sending the "I love that thing" signal. Later, we can change her behavior when she is near the trigger by asking for a *sit* or a *settle*.

Socializing and classical conditioning prevent having to do a lot of desensitizing and counter-conditioning and are done to help the dog avoid developing a negative association with things she is meeting for the first time, as opposed to undoing a negative emotional response already in place. For example, if we take the myriad baby gizmos that your dog may not have seen previously, and introduce her to these things by placing a string of treats on the floor around and leading up to the gizmo, she will likely look at these things and say, "Hum, that's strange and it seems to come with treats—yeah!" or something to that effect.

If your dog is already fearful, we have to go slowly in terms of taking her closer to the object or extending the length of time she is exposed to it. It is important to allow your dog to move toward and away from the new object, at her discretion. Like all of us, she will feel more comfortable around the scary object when she can control how close she is to it. Patience is essential for this.

Often people recommend *flooding*—exposing the dog to triggers up close and without regard for the dog's state of mind, saying, "Just force him and he will see it's not scary." Although this may work on rare occasions, the majority of the time the dog will walk away more fearful.

If you have a dog who is already barking at the dancing baby toys (or maybe even the baby), move her to a distance where the reactivity is no longer happening—no more barking or growling. At this point, your fearful dog is subthreshold (meaning she can tolerate the trigger without reacting), and you can begin to counter-condition and change her emotion around the trigger. Still at the point where there is no reactivity, you will say, "Look at that"—sometimes I go with "What's that?"—as you deliver super-high-value treats. Regardless of what you say, it should always be in a happy tone, which allows us to convey the following: "I see the scary trigger, too. Not to worry and thanks for not reacting. I have your back and oh, yeah, here's a piece of cheese." Because dogs don't technically speak our language, it is difficult to convey all this in conversation as we would with a person who is fearful. But for your dog, that simple phrase is going to become conditioned to mean that she is safe, good things are coming, and there is no need to react. You might then try to get a behavior like a *sit* or see if she

TRAINING TIPS

wants to move away from the trigger entirely. You have to respect what she needs in order to move things along to a point at which she no longer fears the object at any distance.

From there, as the fear or arousal around the trigger lessens, you can build more complicated behaviors by asking your dog to go away from the dancing baby toy with a *go sniff* command, and then build a *sit, down, settle* chain of commands once her fear or arousal is low enough. The behaviors you choose should be based on what your dog can easily do in that particular situation, such as go into another room, just *sit* for a minute, or *settle* next to you for a while.

★ **Proofing behaviors** refers to testing or putting your dog's reactions to commands to the proof. During proofing, try commands in various new situations, with increasing distractions, to see if your dogs really have reliable behaviors. Dogs don't generalize as well as humans, or perhaps they generalize differently. Once you teach your dog to *sit*, you have to understand that does NOT mean she will *sit* anywhere, anytime—it means you have started the process and need to proof that *sit* for every variation you can think of. Practice asking her to perform her behaviors in different locations and circumstances, using consistent reinforcement in all of them.

Once you have proofed her behaviors in a variety of environments and situations while rewarding consistently, you can then begin to randomly decrease the frequency of the reward/treat. You want to get your reward frequency to an intermittent and random schedule so your dog cannot predict when she will be getting her reward. If the behavior is faster, more precise, or just better, it's important to reward your dog, regardless of where you are in the intermittent schedule. This will increase the dog's performance because she will work harder to get the reward the next time. Once the behavior is as reliable as you need, the rewards become com-pletely random and eventually fade out for most commands. Some commands are complicated enough to require intermittent rewards forever, like *settle* in new environments and **come**.

☆ Increasing distance is a subset of proofing, but it is slightly different in that we need to adjust our training to teach the dog to perform commands six, ten, or more feet away—even in another room.

Try playing the toss-the-treat game to build distance. You give the dog a basic command and when she complies (no matter where), you toss a treat/reward far away so she has to go get it. Keep doing this and the dog, being a smart animal, will eventually stay at a distance when perform-ing the command because she figures out that is where the treat will be delivered. With some practice, you have a dis-tance command.

You can also use the baby gates to work on distance commands because they keep the dog from coming toward you while you move farther and farther away as you ask for behaviors.

☆ Group commands are essential for multiple-dog house-holds with children. You will want to start by making sure that each dog knows his or her commands individually. Then work two dogs at a time (if you have more than two, rotate who works with whom). Build a group name like All Dogs, Guys, Girls, Puppies, or whatever you like. Say the group name and reward each dog. Once they are hap-pily responding to their group name, you can give them simple group commands like "All Dogs, *sit*." Ideally, they will all *sit*. If one *sits* first, that dog gets the treat first, but don't wait for the second dog to comply to reward both.

TRAINING TIPS

Rewarding the first sitting dog first will speed up the second dog the next time around. Practice all the commands your dogs know this way so that when things are getting out of hand or you are short on time, you can simply give one command and have everyone follow it.

CHAPTER TWO

Three Dogs
and a Baby

....

With Indy safely in another room being fawned over by his aunties, Lawrence and I were able to greet the dogs with reckless abandon. They bounced, whined, moaned, and ran in circles. Porthos leapt straight up in the air, lifting his eighty-five-pound body completely off the floor several times. Pinball alternated between a groveling scoot while squeaking and also leaping with all four paws off the floor—it's not as incredible when a thirty-pound dog does it. Boo, however, bumped into so many things as he tried to complete his happy dance that it was easier to take him outside and greet him where there was nothing for him to crash into. We let them all accost us to their hearts' content, with all the expected exuberance of dogs who had been away from us for three weeks. My friends (a.k.a. "the aunties") were more than happy to occupy Indy for as long as I needed them to, so the dogs played and greeted me unencumbered until they exhausted all their frustration, exuberance, and joy, while Lawrence returned to the daunting chore of unpacking our car that had barely had enough room for its passengers. Lawrence and I had ridden squeezed between baby items too numerous to count, even in the front seat. The only one with a big comfy seat for the ride was tiny eight-and-a-half-pound Indy in his relatively enormous car seat.

It probably took more than half an hour for the dogs to decompress and begin to behave a bit more normally. Then I visited with my friends and the baby for some time. After everyone had gone and the dogs were calm, I sat in the chair the dogs knew as mine with Indy in my arms and had Lawrence let each dog into the living room, one at a time. Each one came to see me and then caught a whiff of something new, something very different. This organized greeting was designed to allow each dog some individual time with me while I guided them in an appropriate investigation of this new little human in their midst. I held Indy so the dogs could sniff his capped head and his diapered butt effortlessly, keeping my hands in strategic spots so I could easily reach my hand between each dog's nose and Indy if the sniffing became too energetic.

Boo was the first to enter because he had the most experience with kids. While he couldn't see the little bundle in my arms, he clearly sensed something very interesting was right in front of him. I could tell by the way he sped up his pace on approach and his nose went a bit up in the air, moving back and forth, searching to catch the new scent. It reminded me of trying to walk through a darkened house and reaching a hand out in search of obstacles. Once Boo got to me he poked his nose around, gently looking for the new smell, and upon finding it he did his usual snuzzling of Indy with his typical Boo-thusiasm (tender excitement). "Snuzzling" is a word we made up because Boo half snuggles and half nuzzles. Starting with Indy's feet, Boo moved up Indy's back and ended with the baby's cap, at which point I could almost see a joyful light of recognition go on in Boo's head that reminded me so much of the times Boo would visit children on our therapy visits. Boo's investigation of Indy continued as he searched for an ear (Boo was famous for his ear snuzzles). Having located an ear, Boo's examination became just a little intense for a newborn and I had to put my hand in between Boo and Indy. Boo was very happy about the new baby and I believed that if Boo could speak, he would have said, "At last, I have a little boy of my own!"

Porthos was next. He was as human friendly as Boo, just bigger. His experience with children was much more limited than Boo's, but Porthos's approach to Indy was easy and gentle—for an eighty-five-pound dog he was very skilled at being soft while he clearly showed interest. Porthos was more of a specific scent grabber—he would concentrate on a spot and lightly sniff, sniff, sniff until it seemed he had taken in all the smell he could to catalogue it for later. If he could talk, he would have said, "This is pretty nifty, and am I right in thinking this thing makes poop? Excellent." I was very glad Porthos was happy and soft with a newborn one-tenth his mass because at his size Porthos could easily cause injury with the simplest of innocent mistakes.

And last came Pinball—the dog who was small and cute enough to look like the safest but was extremely bad at curbing his energy and quick to jump. Pinball gently sniffed the baby but seemed to show the least amount of intensive investigation. I had to wonder if Pinball was saying something like, "Okay, so what exactly does this thing do?" (At ten days old, babies don't do much that could interest a dog save the production of poop.)

The greetings were as good as I could have hoped—each dog's interaction was happy and interested and ended with no display of conflict or confusion over the baby. But I knew it was not nearly enough—there was more work to be done. Each day as Indy developed and did something new and/or different, the dogs would have to readjust.

And they were not alone. Everyone in the house had to get used to new things, like some sleep deprivation due to the middle-of-the-night feedings and diaper changes. On one level it was a bit easier for the dogs because they could make up any missed sleep during their multiple middle-of-the-day naps. But on another level it was harder for them because I wasn't sure what they understood about Indy's crying. Luckily none of them had an over-the-top reaction to Indy's crying. It was Boo who seemed most disturbed by it. During that first week after Indy arrived, Boo would get up from his pillow, feel his way over to the bassinet, and lean against it whenever Indy cried. As blind and slow as Boo was, he still got there before I could. I have no idea what Boo was trying to do, but knowing Boo, it was a good bet that in his own way he was trying to help. In contrast, Porthos and Pinball would just lift their heads as if to say, "You got that, right?" and then go back to sleep. Not unlike Lawrence and me when we would trade off middle-of-the-night feedings.

People often take these nonchalant behaviors or Boo's seeming concern as a "good sign" that the dogs like the baby. It is tempting to overlay our emotions on our dog and say, "Oh, my dog loves my baby, see, she's not disturbed by the crying at all. . . ." This is quite possible, but there could be other reasons for the behavior, too. The dogs could be disturbed by the crying because of their sensitive ears, given how piercing a baby's cries can be. It is not uncommon for some dogs to respond to things that make them uncomfortable by looking away, being still, and acting disinterested—à la Turid Rugaas's "calming signals," we could have been seeing a look-away, combined with lying down and a yawn here and there—three calming signals clustered together. The best and safest approach was to observe and remain dispassionate about our dogs' reactions to Indy.

Being able to read your dog's signals accurately is essential to keeping her safe around the baby so you can ultimately keep the baby safe. Too many horror stories start with, "The dog was just fine with the baby until . . ."

It's important to remember that what we think is "just fine" is often the dog trying to tell us that the situation is too much for her and she needs our help.

Some of the biggest mistakes I have seen when I am called into a baby-dog situation are born of the owner not understanding the dog's discomfort, confusion, and in some cases terror around this new little critter who neither looks nor acts like a dog, or a human as most dogs know them. I was called into one couple's home when their baby was just six weeks old. Their little dog was quite reactive to their newborn—barking every time someone picked up the baby and growling, lunging, and barking when the baby was in the swing or on the sofa (a large sectional that had the surface area of a bed). They had done everything they had been told to do and the result was a dog who was going to harm the baby if we didn't set things right.

They were given a blanket from the hospital for Dad to bring home so their dog could sniff it and get used to the baby's scent before Mom and Baby came home. The reality is that with 250 million scent receptors, your dog has already smelled that baby on anyone who has handled him or her in the hospital, and potentially has already become familiar with the baby's scent through the mother while the baby was growing. There are a few cases, like mine, where the dog would have no previous exposure to the baby's scent.

The hospital blanket with Baby's scent was really just a placebo for the parents at best and a toy for the dog at worst. If you think about what usually happens in your dog's head when you bring something home and give it to her, then giving a dog a baby-scented blanket could be one of the worst ideas ever. Normally when you present your dogs with a soft, plushy thing, it is a toy, and some dogs may play with it, carry it around, or eviscerate it. But none of them will think, "Oh, this represents something unseen that I will have to be careful around or patient with later on."

On the least worrisome end of the spectrum, your dog sniffs the baby's blanket and thinks, "Oh that's new." But on the other end of the spectrum, your dog takes the baby blanket, runs through the house with it, chewing it and eventually settling in to tear it apart. More than a dozen times a year, newborns or toddlers are killed by their family's dog—let's let your dog meet your baby as a baby, not as something that smells like a toy she got yesterday. Your dog will get enough of the baby's scent once he or she is home, and then it is all about how you introduce the dog to the baby and how you handle the dog when around the baby that will truly allow for bonding and safety down the road.

Unsurprisingly for my clients, the blanket did nothing to help the introductions once Baby was home. A friend of theirs had suggested they put Baby on the sofa and let the dog sniff him first thing when they got home. Placed on this huge sofa, Baby looked like he was floating in the middle of a couch ocean that had previously been the domain of the little dog. About the same size of the newborn, this dog immediately postured with stiff legs and hair up (hackles), barking and lunging. She was instantly punished. From that initial meeting the dog's worst fears were confirmed—Baby was indeed scary and when in the presence of Baby she would be punished.

We assume our dogs understand and see the world the same way we do because we have a relationship with them and many times they do seem to understand us. However, that apparent understanding varies so much from dog to dog and situation to situation that it is impossible to rely on it alone to ensure our dogs will love and be careful around our children. Your dog's ability to discern many different cues from you and her ability to bond with you does not guarantee that she will understand that you don't want her growling or barking at your baby, or that she shouldn't be afraid of this new stranger in her life. Remember the dog who growls is saying, "I don't like that," or, "That scares me," and is giving us an opportunity to intervene before something happens that we cannot undo.

This little dog was not given an introduction that she could handle with instruction and guidance from her owners. She was left to figure things out on her own. From her point of view this baby was unwelcome, and those feelings were reinforced by the angry words from her humans. The good news is that for this family, things did get better. We set up management, training, and guidance protocols, and at last report about a year later, dog and Baby were doing well.

I reintroduced my dogs to Indy each day as I let them spend time with him and me (one or two dogs at a time). At two weeks, Indy could barely make out faces, so to him the dogs were probably just a smelly, warm, panting presence. These encounters were more for the dogs than for Indy. I would feed Indy with one dog *settled* at my feet in the living room. I would change him with one or two dogs hanging out, or read to him with both Porthos and Pinball *settled* at my feet in the nursery. Any Indy-sniffing was limited to when he was in my arms and always ended on a positive note so I could praise the dogs. All these practices allowed the dogs to be a part of Indy's life in a calm, controlled manner and let me praise each dog for being good around the baby so they hopefully understood what I wanted from them around Indy.

People want to believe their dog is a good dog and usually they are right. However, even the nicest person has a blowup every now and then. So just as a good person isn't perfect, having a good dog does not mean you have a perfect dog and it does not mean that your dog won't have a blowup occasionally. Your dog is still an entity who communicates and makes decisions as a dog—not a person. You have to look at what the dog is ethologically (when studied under natural conditions) and compare that to what you want. When there are conflicts or missing pieces regarding what you want and what your dog is, or does, it is your job not to gloss over them but to negotiate the conflicts and provide the missing pieces through training, management, or redirection.

Adult dogs will easily growl at a puppy to say, "Hey, little dog, don't do that." They could air-snap at a puppy or even put the puppy in their mouth for a kind of correction. I knew one German Shepherd mama who growled at her puppy when he tried to nurse long after weaning. When the puppy ignored the growl, he found his whole head held firmly in his mother's mouth just long enough to make a point. Being a puppy, he held still for this correction and no harm was done. Once she let go of him, he shook it off and trotted away to find something else to do. We forget that even if our dogs do understand how fragile human children are, their natural communication signals can be scary and dangerous even when no harm is intended. I never want to squelch a warning like a growl lest I have to deal with the dog who says to himself, "Okay, the growl didn't work," or "I can't use a growl, so I have to ramp things up."

A dog who growls at your baby is not necessarily a bad dog—he is a dog who needs your assistance to make a good choice. And even good dogs can make horrible mistakes. It is our responsibility to set everyone up for success.

In April 2012, the *Las Vegas Review-Journal* reported a

story about Onion—a six-year-old, one-hundred-and-twenty-pound Mastiff-Ridgeback cross—who was by all reports a good dog. His family stated that he had never growled at anyone and had been a source of support for his owner when she went through cancer treatments. The owner's son, the father of Jeremiah Eskey-Shahan, stated, "The dog licks [Jeremiah's] face. He never growls, never snaps at him. I never thought that dog would do anything to my baby." On Jeremiah's first birthday, after a long day of opening presents and even playing with his buddy Onion at grandma's house, where Onion lived, Jeremiah was on the floor and crawled over to the dog. As he had done so many times before, Jeremiah started to pull himself up by the dog's fur. In an instant, Onion grabbed the baby by the head and within thirty seconds had delivered fatal injuries to the boy. The boy's father offered a warning for other families with dogs and babies. "Always be careful, even if you trust your dog," he said. "I trusted my dog, and now I don't have a baby or a dog."

This is a difficult story to read and to tell. The tragic reality is that it happens more than a dozen times a year, yet most, if not all, of these fatalities are preventable. As in this case, it is never an option to allow a baby to crawl on a dog or use the dog to pull himself up, no matter how many times the baby may have already done it. The dog could be hurt by, startled by, or just fed up with this and lash out. This case is also a cautionary reminder that the majority of dog-bite injuries are caused by normally friendly dogs who know or live with the family of their victims—77 percent of biting dogs belong to the victim's family or friends. The takeaway from this statistic is not to fear all friendly dogs, but to remember that when a baby and dog are interacting, our hands need to be precisely where the baby is—not across the room—so we can quickly and easily remove the baby, or the dog, to break up unwanted interactions.

Training Tips You Can Try at Home

★ Dog body language
★ No baby blanket from the hospital
★ Growling: good or bad?
★ When allowing a dog to greet a baby

★ **It is essential to understand dog body language** in order to "hear" what your dog is telling you before the dog feels that he has to resort to a growl or other bigger display to convey his message. As kinetic communicators, dogs rely on their body language to communicate most of what they have to say to each other and to us. People like Turid Rugaas (author of *On Talking Terms with Dogs: Calming Signals*), along with other ethologists, have begun deciphering canine nonverbal communication. It is easy for dog owners to learn enough of the fundamentals of dog body language to keep their baby safe. Some of the basic signals below mean that a dog needs help in a given situation.

☆ **Tail tucked:** A tail tucked under the body means the dog is fearful.

☆ **Tail up:** A tail way up means the dog has made a choice to action (fight or flight).

» A wagging tail means the dog is activated—not unlike the hum of an engine indicates that it is on. (Don't confuse this with the unmistakable happy-hula tail wag, in which the dog's whole backside is going around in a circle like a hula dancer. That is a decidedly happy dog.)

TRAINING TIPS

» The vertical position of the tail is much more important than the wagging (except for the hula-tail). Most individuals bitten by a dog report, "The dog was wagging his tail." They probably didn't notice where it was vertically, which would have given some of the needed warning.

☆ **The look-away:** The dog turns his whole head away from you to politely ask you to please stop or dial back whatever scary thing is happening to or around him, not because he is being rude, doesn't see you, or is "stupid."

☆ **The whale eye (called the half-moon eye in Canada):** This means the dog's eyes are in the corners of their sockets so the whites are showing. Sometimes when a dog is offering a look-away and nothing seems to be changing, he might then offer a whale eye. This dog is trying to maintain the polite head turn while keeping a closer eye on whatever is scary or upsetting. A whale eye is often a prelude to a growl, snarl, or bite.

☆ **Stillness:** A dog who seems to be doing nothing in an active situation is sometimes telling us there is a problem. Being still from head to tail is not a typical action for most dogs. A still dog probably wants to be left alone or is trying to figure things out. When stillness occurs, we should be asking ourselves and the dog (by assessing the rest of the dog's body language), why is this occurring? What's going on? Is the dog resting? Then leave him alone. Is the dog still because he is trying to figure out or defuse something intimidating? If so, we need to address or help him with whatever is frightening. When a dog is still, it is often interpreted as a dog who is "fine" with everything, but a dog who is "fine" will engage with any of the following: a happy open mouth, moving face, curvy and wriggly body and legs offset, while

TRAINING TIPS

sniffing and investigating. A still dog is often a worried dog, and if that worried dog goes from still to stiff, there could be a snarl, growl, or bite on the way.

☆ **Stiff dog:** This dog has gone from being still to stiffening up. His mouth will be closed, eyes harder and fixed, body straight like an arrow, legs usually squared up, and it will seem like all his muscles are tightened up as if readying for fight or flight—and they are. This dog should not be approached.

★ **No baby blanket from the hospital** is necessary. Your dog's ability to smell is another book entirely, and she will usually take care of the smell portion of the baby introduction on her own—from near or far. Giving her a baby blanket can send an incorrect message to a dog who shreds all her toys, or can send no message at all to a dog who is nonplussed by the blanket and disregards it. It does nothing for the relationship between the dog and the baby and may actually set the dog up for a misunderstanding.

Regardless of whether your dog knows the scent of your baby because you have carried it for forty weeks, or doesn't know the scent of your baby because this baby has been adopted or is being fostered, you need to set up baby and dog for success by taking time to allow the dog to adjust to the baby. Try letting her sniff the baby, guided by you with the baby in your arms. Your dog and your baby will be living together for a long time—there is no need to rush the introduction. There is, however, a need to be sure it goes well, no matter how long that might take.

★ **Growling: good or bad?** Let's say something has gone wrong and the dog began barking or growling at the baby. We need to avoid

TRAINING TIPS

punishment in these instances because it will increase the dog's anxiety and reinforce any negative feelings the dog has about the baby.

A dog who is barking or growling at a baby is usually afraid or possibly in some kind of predatory mode. If the dog is reacting because he is afraid and we punish him, we will increase his fear and ensure he has a bad relationship with the baby. If the dog is in predatory mode and we punish, we could overlay fear onto the predatory impulses and increase his reactions. It is also possible he won't even register the punishment unless it is HUGE because predatory instincts often override other input.

When a growl occurs, always REDIRECT—call the dog out of the situation and then manage him. Punishment makes us think we are doing something and accomplishing something, but it is only adding fuel to the fire and setting your baby up for increased risk.

★ **When allowing a dog to greet a baby,** especially a newborn, it is essential that the dog has a calm greeting, so pick the time of day when this is most likely. Typically, dogs are most active and energized at dawn and dusk (they are crepuscular) so the best time for directed dog-baby greeting is the middle of the day.

☆ Slow acclimation—little by little—is the best remedy if your dog is too excited to greet the newborn in your arms. Allow your dog to participate in ritual activities like diaper changing, feedings, and story time. Participating means she would *sit* or lie *down* while you and the baby take care of these activities. All she has to do is be in the room and not be overly excited. Remember, your dog has a lifetime to adjust to this little person. Take your time.

☆ During the calm greeting, your hands should always be within inches of the dog's nose so you can easily insert your hand between your dog and your baby. That way, if your dog gets a little too excited, you can prevent licking or nibbling (dogs often nibble things out of curiosity or affection). An innocent theft of a newborn's hat or nibbling on a tasty piece of baby clothing often has parents wondering if the dog was trying to bite the child or if the child was actually grazed by teeth, and may end with the dog being punished for just being curious. Any of those results in the breakdown of the relationship we want to build through a calm greeting.

Additionally, a dog's tongue is filled with bacteria a newborn cannot protect against, so licking a newborn's face and hands is not an option. Licking of the feet at the early stages is okay, when they cannot put their feet in their mouths yet, but I would rather not see any licking of a newborn. There will be time for this later if you do things right in the beginning.

☆ You also want your hands right there between the dog and baby for introductions so the baby does not put his hands and fingers into the dog's mouth, pull fur, poke the dog's eyes, or smack her upside the head. These actions on the part of the child are not intended to offer insult or do harm but could cause your dog to become fearful of your baby or react in an inappropriate way.

CHAPTER THREE

Colic, Earaches, and Dogs—Oh My . . .

A s Indy settled into his new life with us, he had some hurdles that kept us (including the dogs) awake and exhausted all the time. Right around week four, he began his rapid descent into colic and developed a double ear infection. He slept for no longer than an hour and a half at a time, day or night, and screamed when he was picked up, when he ate, and when we needed to sleep. One of the few things that settled him was a good patting on the back to the beat of ABBA's "Dancing Queen." He was a nine-pound bongo across my lap and reminded me of a comment from my colleague, the president of the local shelter where I consult.

"All dogs love a good pounding," she would say as she played a similar bongo on the back ends of many of the dogs who lived there.

Indy, like those dogs, really did love his "poundings," too. I don't think Lawrence and I will ever listen to ABBA the same way again. One night in particular when Indy was having an extremely bad time of it and I tried to play "Dancing Queen" on the TV sound system, Lawrence said, "I can't listen to it again."

I reminded him that the choice was screaming baby or "Dancing Queen" a couple of times until it lulled Indy to sleep. "Dancing Queen" prevailed and, interestingly, Lawrence and I both noted that I had inadvertently classically conditioned the beginnings of a *settle* command for Indy in much the same way as I taught the dogs how to relax on cue. But "Dancing Queen" was probably one of the strangest cues ever used to relax and soothe a baby to sleep. The dogs also seemed to have learned the musical cue and when Indy needed his "Dancing-Queen-Bongo-Baby," as it came to be known, the dogs would simply lie *down* and *settle*, too.

Group settles in general were some of the few moments each dog still had with me since they were left mostly to their own devices during this time. Porthos took this in stride. He simply removed himself to the master bedroom for downtime and reappeared to eat, go outside, and hang out after dinner, and he loved Indy's story time. Boo, too, was happy to nap between outings and eating. He was always in the living room with Indy but couldn't do too many stairs each day, so he opted out of story time.

Pinball was the most put out by the new baby. He had been the baby before Indy arrived and at eighteen months, Pinball was in a critical behavioral/fear period. Wherever I was, Pinball wanted to be there, too, which often left him lying on the other side of a baby gate, watching us with a kind of hopefulness. Even though he was a fairly aggressive resource guarder, we had made great strides in counter-conditioning that behavior. But when faced with the abundance of baby toys, he just couldn't resist stealing them. We were left with the seemingly constant task of buying back stolen toys with a treat or different toy while carrying an infant on one hip. At the time, I wondered if his increased stealing was a grab for attention (good or bad, he didn't care), but in hindsight I realized it was his way of dealing with increased anxiety that he was having a hard time processing. Many times it was easier to send Pinball outside—not the best for training, but definitely a decent management technique. Luckily, we had the fence and he loved to hang out on the deck in all weather—it was the one thing that trumped being wherever I was.

Household management policies were strictly enforced across the board for all dogs. Boo was the only dog allowed to roam free in the living room when Indy was in his bassinet and Lawrence or I had to leave the room to attend to something. As the other dogs demonstrated their ability to be calm and follow directions to *settle* around the baby, they were gradually allowed into the living room off leash, one at a time along with Boo. Porthos was the first to earn this privilege, but Pinball's need to be with me motivated him to follow directions. Soon he, too, earned his right to be in the living room with all of us. However, no matter how good any of them were, it was always Boo and only one other dog at the beginning. It was as if too much biomass in one small room made for a volatile and unstable situation, and by rotating who was allowed in the living room with Indy we were able to avoid a canine meltdown. Whoever was not allowed in with us was left on the other side of the baby gates to *settle*, but I made sure to swap out turns for "happy" baby time. If Porthos and Boo were hanging with us in the living room, then Pinball would be the one to go upstairs with us for the diaper change. Or Pinball and Porthos would come up for story time. The dogs got used to being on the other side of the gates and seemed to understand they would get their turn at baby time. However, it was a happy day when they were relaxed enough around Indy that we only closed the gates when there was too much going on (guests in the house, dog feedings, or Indy's belly time on the floor. In spite of the crying and the colic, the dogs seemed to be adjusting to the new living arrangements, and I think Pinball actually liked his extra outside adventures.

The gates and physical management were the biggest part of the adjustment for us besides life redefined by a baby-in-charge. All our dogs had earned their freedom in the house pretty quickly after being potty-trained and now to have to restrict their movements and access to various parts of the house felt unfair on one level but necessary on another. I knew from the statistics and specific dog-baby tragedies that a baby in someone's arms, in a swing, or in another baby contraption is not necessarily safe if dogs are allowed to be free without learning how to behave around the baby and respond reliably to commands. As a result, I felt it was better to be conservative and restrict the dogs in the short term in order to keep Indy safe and the dogs with us for the long haul. Lawrence agreed with me, but the application of the new rules was often difficult to follow given our sleep deprivation. Luckily, each dog had good foundational skills and even when we forgot to close a gate, it was pretty easy to send a dog out of a room or ask him to lie *down* or *wait* while we organized things.

The thought of physically managing their dogs around their babies raises a host of objections for many people. The first is psychological: "Why do we need gates or crates? Doesn't that mean my dogs are bad in some way?"

No. It means they are dogs and perhaps at times in our lives we have to accept that we cannot manage everything at once. We have no problem locking our cars in a parking lot because we will not be able to stand over them while we shop. We have no issue locking our houses at night because we will be asleep and cannot watch over them. We don't think twice about putting stoppers on cabinet doors or drawers because we can't watch toddlers every second. There are many times when it will simply be impossible to watch baby and dog, keep yourself awake, answer the door, make dinner, take a shower, and do all the other things you need to do. The solution is having a baby gate or two or a dog crate available.

The second objection for many people is often the location and the logistics of gates in a home with an open floor plan; in addition, some parents may simply not like the look of gates. There are a number of gates made for wide spaces. Some are attractive, some expensive, and some basically portable plastic play yards for kids. In the end it is up to you to decorate your home, but the safety of your baby will dictate the setup of your house more than aesthetics. Always remind yourself—it won't be forever. I remember a time not long ago when my living room was not decorated with baby toys and I know in my heart there will be a time again, some day in the future, when it will return to an adult space, but not today. The same goes for the gates.

The last objection I often encounter is probably the easiest to fix—the dog is not happy in another room, in the crate, or on the other side of a gate. This is something we can teach dogs to do happily. Remind yourself that in the short term it may require a bit of training, but in the long term it will pay off. With this training, we can have time that is just for us and the baby, and then, when the dogs are calm, time that includes them in a manner that will allow instruction and learning. Times of chaos are not conducive to teaching or learning.

While our dogs' lives had changed dramatically, as had Lawrence's and mine, they still had a good chunk of their old lives when Indy was napping or when we all retreated to the master bedroom for the night. There the dogs had their usual spots: Pinball in the bed, Porthos in his area of the room on his pillow, and Boo on the pillow next to me. The only change in the room was the addition of the bassinet. The master bedroom had always been neutral ground for the dogs. There had never been wild play or any altercations in there, unlike in the living room that was in effect their rec room. Even Pinball's guarding was less severe up there. Because dogs don't generalize well, it is common to have behaviors that are specific to certain locations or activities.

These location-specific behaviors inform our dog-child management strategies in that we look at the dog's typical behavior in each location or circumstance and manage accordingly. In other words, we say to ourselves, "Is this the room where they always get crazy? Then no dog-baby interactions here."

Or we ask ourselves if we can keep the baby safe while training or guiding the dog. In other words: "Can I actually pay close enough attention to my baby while I train the dog? Or do I need to use a baby gate to let me focus on the baby and then train the dog later?"

These simple questions are often the last ones parents have asked before I am called in for a dog-baby consultation. Yet these questions are the start of establishing household dog-baby policies.

The flip side of all this management is an approach to priorities that will make a lot of folks scratch their heads. Sometimes the best way to ensure you can devote your time to taking care of your baby is to take care of the dogs first. Ear infections are common in babies due to the position of the ear canal in their early years, and often a barking dog can really disturb babies with an ear infection—never mind wake them from that nap you've been struggling to get them to take. One of the first signs that Indy had an ear infection was the day Boo barked and Indy screamed bloody murder. He had previously not cared about barking dogs and since then he has consistently only cared about barking if his ears are bothering him.

Deciding whether to focus first on the dogs or the baby was one of the points of conflict between Lawrence and me. I was more proactive with the dogs and he was more reactive. I would plan ahead to be sure the dogs were out and fed before I brought Indy down or fed him. Lawrence waited for the dogs to tell him they needed something. As with all marriages, we kept working toward a compromise. But in the end, if the dog's gotta pee, the dog's gotta pee—so if I take care of the dog, I won't have to split myself down the middle when taking care of Indy.

• • •

> ## Training Tips You Can Try at Home
>
> ★ *Settle*
> ★ Fear periods (sometimes called "critical fear periods")
> ★ Gates and crates!
> ★ Basic skills
> ★ Integrating training into everyday life
> ★ Taking care of the dog first
> ★ Having to walk dogs while adjusting to a newborn baby

★ *Settle*—this is one of the most important behaviors to teach a dog and yet probably one of the least often taught. It is defined as a relaxed *down* that can be done anywhere and can last from five minutes to an hour. *Settle* is unlike *stay* in that dogs in a *settle* can readjust their position. For example, they can get up and go around in a circle to get more comfortable, scratch, stretch out, and so on, but they cannot leave the imaginary box in which you put them. To start, I usually use a dog pillow, blanket, or towel to mark the area for the *settle*, but over time they should be able to *settle* anywhere on any surface.

☆ Begin with your dog in a *down* and ask her to roll one hip to the side so her body makes a kind of half-moon shape from front paws to back paws with her belly a bit exposed—this will help her relax and she is less likely to pop up from that position. As soon as she flops her hip over, drop treats either between her front two paws or just to her side (on the inside of the curve of her body near her belly). Don't hand the treats to the dog. You want her looking for treats on the floor (not from your hands). This way when she wants more, she will look for it on the floor instead of immediately nudging you or getting up. This will help with duration and distance: she won't feel the need to follow the treat dispenser (you) because there might be one under her leg.

☆ Once you have given the *settle* command, don't repeat the command. Instead, praise your dog right before you drop the treats each time you drop the treats (or you will never be able to fade the treats). If she gets out of the *settle* (probably too much time passed between rewards), I usually wait without giving her another command, from a few seconds up to a minute. The determining factor will be how long your dog continues to look to you to figure out how to keep getting those treats. We want to see if the dog will self-correct and go back into the *settle*. Many dogs do self-correct, realizing the *settle* is where they get continuous good things. If they break the *settle* and do not self-correct after a reasonable wait, walk them around in a little circle and then re-command them—this little circle is sort of like a restart. Then withhold the reward after the re-command until the dog has been in the *settle* for a few seconds. Then keep the rewards flowing as randomly as possible.

If you don't do this restart, your dog could easily figure out, "Okay, I *settle*, then get up, then *settle* again, and I can get my rewards even faster. I could do this all day!"

☆ The *settle* reward schedule should go as follows: In the beginning, treats should be continuous—drop multiple treats in rapid succession. You will want to use your dog's kibble in the beginning to be sure you can be as generous as necessary to ensure a reliable *settle*. After your dog has

TRAINING TIPS

been holding the *settle* for a minute or so, slowly reduce as follows, with as much unpredictability as possible.

» Begin to slow how quickly the treats are being dealt out.

» Then start to reduce the number of treats you toss each time while keeping the number random—sometimes several, sometimes one, then sometimes two, and so on. Your dog should have the same feeling as a person playing a slot machine, never knowing if the next one will be the **big one**.

» While you are randomizing the reward schedule, be sure that you get the treats to your dog before she gets up, and be sure you get those treats near enough to her so she doesn't get up to go get them.

» Your dog will figure out any schedule that is not completely randomized. I had a client who was counting between treat delivery and her puppy picked up on this and started barking right before the delivery was scheduled.

» Generosity in these early stages will allow you to reduce the rewards down to nothing, but being stingy in the beginning will ensure you will need to treat this forever.

☆ To build distance on this *settle*, you will want to drop several treats as you stand up and walk a few feet from the dog and then return to re-treat the dog. Continue this maneuver while adding a little distance at a time, until you can walk out of the room and return to your dog still in the *settle*.

☆ Building duration into a *settle* moves at a steady pace, starting with a few seconds, slowly increasing to a couple of minutes, and working up to half an hour or more after a few weeks. When you will be away from the dog for longer periods and she is still learning the *settle*, leave her with a Kong or other puzzle toy.

☆ If you are starting to teach the *settle* with baby already in the picture, use feeding time and story time to work on *settle*. Because you will already be parked for these activities, it will be easy as long as you have the treats nearby.

Diaper time will be a little trickier because you will be up and moving. Begin adding *settle* to this activity only after you have done a few repetitions in which you are in a more stationary position.

☆ Always end the *settle* with an *all done* command so your dog releases on your command and not when she is bored.

★ **Fear periods** are sometimes also called "critical fear periods" or "fear stages." Although these periods do typically come with increased fears, they also include developmental stages such as independence, sexual maturity, and entry into final adulthood. The fears that show up at these times are some of the most dramatic changes we notice in our dogs. Most of us expect the standard developmental milestones of independence and maturity on a number of levels. However, many pet owners do not expect their fifteen-month dog to suddenly be afraid of a person he has known all his life, as Porthos was with our UPS man whom he had known happily from the time he was seven weeks old.

When faced with a dog going through a fear period, it is important to return to your early socialization with desensitization and counter-conditioning (DS/CC). Your dog's brain has shifted, not unlike a train switching to another track, and he needs you to help him get back on the right one. The behaviors that crop up in fear periods should not be met with punishment but rather assistance in the form of reinforcing the behaviors you like and redirecting or managing the behaviors you do not want.

It is important to note your dog's age when your baby comes home and begins crawling, walking, tossing objects, or running after the dog. If any of these coincide with one of the fear periods below, be sure to redouble your management, training, and DS/CC efforts to get everyone through the period safely.

The timing of the fear periods is as follows, but because of the wide variety in how dogs mature based on their size and breed, there is a flexible margin:

- » Around seven to nine weeks

- » Between five and six months

- » Either side of ten months

- » Twelve to thirteen months

- » Fifteen to eighteen months

- » Eighteen months is usually the last of the official fear stages, but dogs can still be developing through three years, depending on their size, with some accompanying behavioral changes.

★ **Gates and crates!** Parents use gates to keep babies and toddlers safe around fireplaces, stairways, or doorways but often think their dogs should not be "left out."

Gates allow us to set boundaries and keep our babies and dogs safe when we cannot watch them closely. Two-month-old Aiden McGrew of South Carolina lost his life to the family dog, Lucky, when his father fell asleep after putting the child in a baby swing. If Lucky had been on the other side of a baby gate while the father slept, it would have saved that child's life and the father would not have been charged with homicide by child neglect.

☆ Teaching our dogs how to be happy on the other side of a gate or in a crate is pretty easy but will take a bit of attention and training.

» We begin by tossing a treat for our dog before we close the door of the baby gate (or crate) so the dog is on the other side.

» Then treat him for being on the other side of the gate or crate.

» Take a step away, then return and treat him.

» Take enough steps away so you cannot reach him and toss the treat.

» Return to the gate and treat him. Then move farther away and toss the treat. Repeat this rotation of reaching out to hand him a treat and tossing him a treat from farther away. You don't want him thinking you always have to be near the gate or crate for him to get something. He needs to never know when he might get rewarded except that it is when he is on the other side of the gate or in the crate. Once he has figured this out, you can move to the next step.

» Note: If your dog starts to jump or bark, you should turn away, walk away, and IGNORE him. DO NOT TALK to him; DO NOT LOOK at him. As soon as he is quiet, toss the treat. Your dog will figure out quickly that quiet gets him what he wants.

» If your dog will work for his kibble, great. However, if not, you will need a treat that is higher value. For high-value treats, be sure to read the ingredients of the treats and look for treats that have meat as the first ingredient.

» Once your dog is happily standing quietly on the other side of the gate or in the crate, then start asking the dog to *settle* there. Follow the *settle* directions above, adjusting for your being on the other side of a gate or crate.

» At some point, you will walk away from the gate or the crate and go do something. If you will be doing something that won't allow you to intermittently return to the dog to treat him, or you won't be able to toss him a treat—for example, if you are taking a nap or a shower—leave him with a Kong, stuffed bone, or puzzle toy so he is happily occupied while you are otherwise engaged.

» Eventually, when your dog is on the other side of a gate or in the crate, you will no longer need to interact with him because he will be content with that place and not need further assistance.

» If your dog is really opposed to being alone, however, there will be some setbacks. You can always feed him his meals on the other side of the gate or in his crate while you are in another room in addition to working the above steps.

☆ If your dog hurts himself in the crate, you will want to try to build happy crate time, following the steps above but at a much slower pace and only for occasional use. Although you may not envision putting your dog in a crate regularly, there are situations in addition to management that will call for your dog to have crate time: if the dog is lost and taken in by Animal Control, or if the dog is injured or must undergo surgery that requires crate rest for a period of time. If your dog finds himself in either of these situations and is unhappy in the crate, he will be extremely stressed and may hurt himself while crated, and his crate fears will only increase. If your dog simply cannot adjust to a crate, do not force the issue and rely on the gates instead.

☆ Each dog and each dog-baby combination will require different levels of gate usage. For some it will be necessary only in the beginning as your dog earns your trust. For some it will be until your dog and child have shown they can follow the rules together. The measurement of when to stop using gates is not time or age—it is good reliable behavior with kids.

★ **Basic skills** to build a foundation for communicating with and verbally managing your dog are critical with a baby in the home.

» *All done* teaches your dog that the game or activity is over. You will need to provide rewards for the first several weeks whenever you say "*all done.*"

» *Come* should be paid for exceedingly well for the first six months. Jackpot your dog when he gets to you, and when fading rewards, only reduce to intermittent rewards. Your dog should get a reward for *come* every now and then, forever.

» *Down*: Your dog's entire body is lying down; butt, hips, and elbows are touching the floor.

» *Drop it* (some use *give*): Your dog should drop items from her mouth on command. This should be one of the greatest games you ever play with your dog so she loves to give up things (details in Chapter Ten).

» *Go say hello*: Your dog will move forward to greet a person without jumping (details in Chapter Eight).

» *Go sniff*: You can direct your dog away from anything or anyone, including your baby, with a simple hand gesture (details in Chapter Five).

» *Leave it*: Your dog should not go toward, sniff, pick up, or bark at an object that you indicate. In short, this command means "Don't even think about it." (Details in Chapter Ten.)

» *Off*: Your dog should get *off* the counter, the couch, you, your guests, or anything he is on. Do not use *down*. Human language works having one word mean different things in different contexts, but dogs need each command to have one meaning.

TRAINING TIPS

» *Settle*: Your dog should relax on cue in a spot you indicate. See details above.

» *Sit*: Your dog's butt is on the floor. Don't repeat your command. *Sit* is the most often repeated command. This repetition teaches dogs to *sit* on three or four commands or to ignore the command, or it just cranks up their energy.

» *Stand*: Your dog is standing still on all four feet. This command allows you to wipe paws, do tick checks, and make sure your dog doesn't think *sit* is just the beginning of *down* by allowing you to use *stand* between a *sit* and a *down*.

» *Stay*: Your dog is essentially frozen in place. She is at military attention until you release her with the *all-done* command.

» *Wait* is the equivalent of "hang on a second." Your dog should literally pause for two to thirty seconds—it is a short break in your dog's activity.

☆ If you have started this process and your dog knows some of these commands but not reliably, then it is time to review the section on proofing (Chapter One).

☆ If you have not begun to teach commands and already have a baby, don't think it's too late. It is never too late to start training. It will require a little more multitasking to integrate the training into everyday life.

☆ For more information on any of these skills, see blogs and videos at www.threedogstraining.com or www.pleasedontbitethebaby.com.

☆ If you and your dog are still having trouble establishing the above skills, please seek out the help of a professional dog trainer. See Chapter Eight for details on choosing a dog trainer.

★ **Integrating training into everyday life** takes two major commitments and an understanding of successive approximation:

You will need treats in containers all around the house. Some of my clients have thought just one treat pouch is enough. But when you have to feed your baby at two in the morning, you are not going to be in a frame of mind to go looking for the treat pouch—having containers already in place around the house will allow you to ask the dog for various behaviors anywhere.

You will also need a clear idea of what you want to teach your dog. With these commitments, you can train anywhere, anytime, anyplace.

☆ Changing a diaper and dog wants attention? Ask for a *down* and toss a treat as you wipe the poopy butt, or ask for a *go sniff* and toss the treat. Because you have a treat container within reach of the changing table—no problem. Parents and all caretakers of newborns (and older children, too) know how to multitask. This is just another element in the multitasking list.

☆ Nursing or feeding your baby? Ask your dog to *sit* or *down* at your feet and occasionally give him a treat for holding position, and soon you can call it a *settle* by building more duration and a more relaxed posture through successive approximations. Because your treats are in a container within reach—no problem.

"Successive approximation" is a complicated phrase that has a simple concept—reward something that is on the way to the final goal. Then slowly increase the level of performance you are asking of your dog. For example, if your dog won't lie *down*, you could reward the dog for beginning to bend over, then three-quarters of a *down*,

TRAINING TIPS

then one elbow on the floor, then crouched with just a little light showing under the body, and finally the complete *down*. We reward better and better behaviors until we get the final behavior we want. This concept allows us to be free of the need to be perfect so we can relax and integrate training into everyday life.

★ **Taking care of the dog first** sounds crazy. But if we get the dogs fed and get them out for their potty, then we can devote our time to our baby.

☆ Once you have a routine for your child's napping and eating, you can ask yourself, When will my son or daughter be up and need my attention? What is my dog's daily routine? When you have both routines in hand, you can compare and shift things. For example, you can let the dogs out and feed them before baby gets up in the morning or from a late afternoon nap. Or sometimes, you can let the baby play in belly time or in the play yard while you feed the dogs and let them out. The most difficult scenario to process would be when the baby is crying but the dogs are underfoot. I would get the dogs out of the room or house and then attend to the baby, provided I could take care of the dogs quickly—hence the reason for all my training.

If you try to take care of a baby emergency with your dogs underfoot and possibly riled up, the situation could break down into something dangerous.

☆ Sometimes taking care of the dogs before the baby works out perfectly and the schedules match up nicely. However, there will be times when they won't. This then becomes another multitasking time that can be made a bit easier by thinking outside the box. No reason your baby can't be in

the bouncy chair on a kitchen island or counter as you prepare the dog's food. No reason you can't be wearing your
baby in a sling while you take the dogs out.

The easiest solution is to get the dogs done and out of
the way, but sometimes life just doesn't cooperate. At that
point you can creatively combine tasks and through distance and management safely include the baby in your dog
caretaking.

★ I cannot imagine having a newborn and having to walk
three dogs for peeing and pooping several times a day. A fenced-in
yard works for us. But, if you live in an apartment or condo or don't
have a fenced-in yard, reach out to a dog walker to help out with
walking your dog(s) for the first few months after baby arrives. Once
you are comfortable taking your baby out in the stroller with you for
walks, it will be lovely quality time for you, baby, and dog, provided
your dog(s) have good leash-walking skills (more in Chapter Eleven).

TRAINING TIPS

CHAPTER FOUR

Balancing— Pack and Sleep

···

Being sleep-deprived, as so many parents are with a newborn, is never optimal—not for taking care of baby, training dogs, or working full-time as both Lawrence and I were still doing. Luckily, I had flexibility when scheduling my clients and a good portion of the appointments were in the evenings or on Saturdays when most folks were not at work. Lawrence's job was a typical Monday thru Friday daytime job, and he could work from home three or four days a week. When we meshed our schedules, Indy had both of us there most of the time and one of us always. This was great for Indy, but the rest of us (humans *and* dogs) needed more sleep and just a little quiet alone time.

Collectively, we were suffering from trigger stacking—a dog-training term that refers to exposing a dog to various stressors (triggers) one on top of the other. There is no relief from the first trigger before the next one appears. Our house is a log house with open spaces everywhere and no sound insulation. We could have a conversation from opposite ends of the house with only a slight increase in our volume. The office configuration was even worse. When in the nursery for a nap, Indy heard everything I was doing in the office right below—calling clients, opening a file cabinet drawer, or using the printer. Using the electric stapler was a surefire way to wake him up. Going up the stairs that were right outside his room was another. Because sound traveled so easily through the house, collective tiptoeing was required when Indy was napping, and Lawrence and I avoided going up the stairs, lest we wake Indy from his still fragile, colicky sleep.

Another mother had once given me the advice, "Nap when the baby naps." This seems very sound, but Lawrence and I just couldn't lose those precious hour-and-a-half slices of time into which we needed to jam everything that had to be done each day. From conducting business calls or concentrating on work to doing regular household chores, from Lawrence and Lisa quality time to dog quality time, playtime, nail trimming, brushing, or training, it all had to be done at reduced volume.

We were like villagers in a contemporary fairy tale, trying to live our daily lives without waking the sleeping giant during his few hours of sleep each day. Lawrence and I worked on top of each other in the living room—the room farthest from the nursery. Filing was out of the question and my client calls were restricted to when Indy was up and often involved me walking the house using the headset while cradling Indy and playing bongo-baby to keep him from crying.

There was no way for all of us to totally decompress, although the dogs did have a few more places for some quiet than Lawrence and I did. Pinball had the yard to patrol. Porthos had the master bedroom for some solitude once I put down some carpet treads for the stairs to reduce the sound of his paw steps. Boo had his big comfy chair in the living room. But even with those opportunities for some quiet time, the dogs still had trouble sleeping through the colicky crying, and when Indy was napping they were restricted in terms of their usual games—no alert barking at the deer spooking our house, no rough loud play, basically no noise. Because the only solution to our daily walking on eggshells dysfunctional routine was to rebuild the house, which wasn't feasible, the family mantra was "This colic will pass and we *will* sleep again."

It was during this tiptoeing, sleep-deprived delirium that I had to ask myself, "Why *three* dogs?" This question had lurked in the back of my mind and was often asked by friends, clients, and family. It made sense at the time we got Boo. Atticus was ten years old and slowing down. Dante was clearly a dog who would need canine companionship after Atticus passed. And I probably needed another dog to volunteer with as Dante got older. I figured having three was a good plan. It all seemed so right until Porthos entered the picture, and then because of his medical and behavioral complications we began to doubt this logic. Pinball caused us to say out loud: "Two would be good." But it wasn't until there was a baby human in the mix that we saw how hard it was going to be with *these* three.

I beat myself up for not being able to provide a better life for the dogs, Indy, and even Lawrence and me, but I ultimately came back to the realization that every family faces hurdles. Although our issues might have seemed odd to some and might even have been dismissed as reckless by others, we had been chosen to parent this wonderful child because of our home and our animals. It was therefore my job to find the positive and make life for Indy and the dogs as good as I could. In an odd way, the pressure of *these* three dogs worked in our favor because we never entertained the idea that the dogs would all be fine. We knew it was going to require training, management, and guidance for everyone. With fewer dogs (or maybe different dogs), it would have been easy to say, "Oh, we only have one or two dogs, so everything will be fine. They are good dogs and they love us, so they will love our baby." Too many horror stories and broken hearts have resulted from this attitude.

One such story tells of a six-year-old girl who was out playing alone with her family's friendly Golden Retriever. In only a few unaccompanied minutes, the dog fatally strangled the girl by playing tug-of-war with her scarf. The chief of the Suffolk County Society for the Prevention of Cruelty to Animals, interviewed after this incident, repeated a dangerous attitude when he stated, "There was probably a one-in-a-million chance for something like this to happen."

Statistically, the chance of being killed by a dog is around 1 in 150,000, much higher than any of us like to think. To me, this tragic incident with the six-year-old and her Golden Retriever lies at the heart of the issues we face when we have dogs and kids living together—even the most loving and friendly dog is powerful and can make deadly mistakes.

Like a doctor trying to convey the gravity of a potential illness without panicking the patient, as a trainer I have to carefully let parents know about the things that need to be changed, avoided, or managed for the sake of safety. A few months after Indy was born, I was in the home of clients with a tiny two-month-old baby girl and a big eighty-five-pound dog who was tall enough to hover over the floor swing and easily stick his head in to reach the baby. I pointed out their dog's head was at the right height to lick the baby and transfer germs she may not be ready to fight off, and suggested that the dog might also be tempted to take items out of the swing, like toys or snacks. It would have only flooded the parents with fear and probably immobilized them if I had told them about the possibility of the baby being pulled out of her swing and killed by the family dog. It can be hard to know when parents need to hear about these incidents to help them make better management decisions or when these stories will simply cause them to turn to denial or kick their dog to the curb in a knee-jerk reaction.

Belly time, floor time, swings, and gadgets on the floor are all part of newborn life. The question of how to handle these moments with dogs in the house has many answers. One such answer is not to have the gadgets at all, but that is hard to do and not good for babies because they need these enrichment opportunities. Another answer may be to use movable play yards to encase the swing or baby on the floor so the dogs simply cannot access the baby. Alternatively, parents can be sure to always be within reach of the baby when the dog is also in the room so they can intervene if the dog gets too interested or too aroused. The third answer is, of course, easier with one dog. More than one dog might require different stages of gates and other physical management to create different zones in the house. This allows parents to separate the dogs from the baby and each other in order to train one dog at a time to *settle* while the baby rolls around on the floor or begins to crawl. These answers are actually pretty simple, but parents often don't ask the question in the first place.

Many of us remember the days when seat belts were not mandatory and our mother's arm was the only safety device between us and the windshield, or when only a true nerd would dare wear a bicycle helmet. These two safety measures are now legally mandated, not because everyone was having traffic accidents but because they are simple ways to prevent the terrible outlying injuries that can take thousands of lives or leave people disabled. For my client with the eighty-five-pound dog, gates were essential, and for the little girl and her Golden Retriever, the rule of supervise-as-if-your-dog-is-a-swimming-pool would have saved her life. Once we start asking the questions, the answers are straightforward and effective.

Indy had belly time in the living room with Boo free in the room only if we were right there next to him. Being blind, Boo could easily have stumbled on Indy, which could have been upsetting for both of them even without any intent to do harm. But with us there, Boo could be guided to gently snuzzle Indy and we could be sure no baby was stepped on by the blind but very loving Boo. Indy also had belly time in the play yard, with Pinball and Porthos allowed and encouraged to hang out around the perimeter to make positive associations with being around Indy. Even with all these steps toward management, the gates, the fence, and decent basic commands, we still had to deal with Pinball, who was stealing more and still giving us the "I'll bite you" whale eye when we needed to get a baby toy from him. I have a picture of him that I use regularly in classes to demonstrate the whale eye, in which Pinball is holding a pair of open scissors in his mouth. If captioned, it would read, "Don't come near me or I'll cut you!"

When Pinball wasn't stealing, he was a sensitive, snuggly, affectionate dog who was exceedingly good at his basic skills and some really cute tricks. He was also so good with other dogs that he started working alongside me with my clients whose dogs were fearful of people but not dogs. In this role, Pinball was stellar. He gently guided the other dogs to play and interact with him, then the other dog would associate me with Pinball and soon I was in that dog's circle of friends. These clients adored Pinball for being his affectionate self but also for the joy he brought their dogs. My ongoing challenge as his owner and trainer was to help him to be more comfortable with strangers in our house while I worked to control his resource guarding. If nothing else, I was developing a specialty in severe resource guarding.

In a typical twist of fate for us, while I questioned my abilities to get Pinball to be a safe and integrated member of our household, I found that my other training skills (honed by so many crate-trained puppies) paid off at this point in Indy's development. It was around three and a half months that one night Lawrence got up during one of Indy's middle-of-the-night crying sessions and handed me the baby, saying only, "Hold him." Lawrence proceeded to disassemble the Pack 'n Play, move it into the nursery, and reassemble it in his sleepy haze. He then retrieved Indy from me and deposited him in his own bed in his own room (right across the hallway). I could not argue. We all needed sleep.

We listened to Indy carefully and watched him on the baby monitor that was hooked up to all our portable devices. We could see him on our iPhones or iPad and know that he was in the right position and safe or if he needed us. Then we started applying standard crate-training principles. If he occasionally cried, we timed it—all the while watching on the iPhone. We gave him ten minutes to self-soothe—which seemed like a cruel eternity—but he usually did soothe himself back to sleep and if not, we responded. I knew I had to allow him to work it out himself or I would be reinforcing waking at all hours.

When I describe crate training for puppies to some of my clients, they say, "Oh, we are Ferberizing the puppy!"

We both laugh when I say, "No, we are crate training the baby."

Soon, we began to recognize the "one-off" cries, wherein Indy would wake and then be able to calm himself back to sleep, versus the "I really, really need something" cries, at which point we would go to him. This strategy worked like a charm, and from about fourteen weeks on, he slept through the night. Even with all the guilt about having these dogs in this baby's life swirling around, I was able to say "It's good to have dogs" because their training had enabled me to give us all the gift of sleeping through the night by essentially crate-training the baby.

I also applied some of my conditioning techniques to a few of Indy's daily scheduled events to build happy routines out the yin-yang. We had story time every night before bed to build good bedtime habits, which were essential for solid sleep habits later on. There were after-breakfast songs and dances while I had to do boring things like dress or make the bed—ensuring I had a few songs, besides "Dancing Queen," to which Indy would automatically respond to happily, including the theme song to *Jeopardy!* Most nights Indy's regular feeding took place around the same time as *Jeopardy!* He was quickly conditioned to smile when he heard that tune. Bath time, too, was a festival. In the early days, before Indy was big enough to sit up safely in the tub alone, either Lawrence or I would be with him in our swimming suits in the oversized Jacuzzi tub that we had not used more than once before in all the thirteen years we'd lived here. I finally knew why the universe had given us that crazy tub. Soon Indy was big enough to sit up on his own and he could be alone in the smaller tub. We made a point to make everything we could silly and fun. Even diaper changes included silly songs, weird faces, and funny noises—the diaper-changing battle was not a battle I wanted to have. All the things I needed him to be comfortable with later on or happy doing for a while as he matured became the funniest, silliest games we could make them.

• • •

Training Tips You Can Try at Home

★ Sleeping through the night, or crate training for babies
★ Gates versus play yards, where and when one is better
★ Resource Guarding

★ **Sleeping through the night, or crate training for babies,** is a little bit Skinnerian and a little bit Ferber. Like puppies, babies can begin to learn to sleep on their own longer and longer each night if they are allowed to self-soothe.

Usually, as soon as I put Indy down, the crying would begin and I would check my watch, telling myself if he kept crying for ten minutes I would get him and see if I could soothe him to sleep. By timing the crying and letting him learn to relax on his own, I was kept from overreacting and teaching him that fussing was a good thing. It sounds clinical, but when we started timing Indy's crying, what seemed like an eternity was usually never more than seven minutes and mostly he was settled after four or five minutes. As a result, we ended up with a baby who could play happily by himself in his nursery before falling asleep or upon waking up. This gave us the time we needed to feed ourselves, dress ourselves, take care of the dogs, or even do some work. Although I started with ten minutes and figured I'd have to tweak it one way or the other, after about a week there was usually no need to time it anymore. When we put him down to nap or to bed for the night, he had an established routine and typically within three minutes he was playing himself to sleep or already sleeping.

★ **Gates come in handy** for belly time, but I prefer a play yard. The play yard allows you to let your baby have belly time in any room where you might be. Play yards can go to grandma's house, out in the backyard on a nice day, or even to the park. Your baby can enjoy a little freedom to explore when he or she may not be ready for the whole room, and you can be beside your baby or go ahead and answer the phone without worrying about where the dog is. Movable play yards let your dog(s) get used to your baby in a variety of places in and out of the house. They can also watch the baby a little more closely as he or she does baby things. Your dogs need to see how this child moves and what he or she does in order to begin to process what and who they are as a part of their family.

☆ You can use play yards around swings, for belly time, or even when the baby begins taking those tottering first steps and you need to take care of personal or household chores and can't be closely monitoring the dog and the baby together.

☆ Belly time without gates or play yards is an option only suitable for when you are right next to the baby to oversee the dog's interaction with him or her. Ideally, the dog would be in a *down* position and *settled* out of reach of the newborn as he or she squiggles, wriggles, and rolls. It would be easy for a dog to mistake a baby on the floor for something to be played with like a dog toy, so sniffing and hovering over the baby would only be appropriate with your hands between them. Letting your dog spend quality time with you and your baby in this managed manner can be a nice bonding exercise.

TRAINING TIPS

★ **Resource guarding** refers to a dog's behavior when she guards food, toys, bones, or other resources. Most dogs will guard something at some point in their lives, but not all of them qualify as a resource guarder. The dog who earns the resource-guarding distinction will go to extremes, such as showing teeth, growling, and potentially biting someone who tries to take her "stuff."

☆ Owners are often told to show their dog who is boss and take away the dog's objects, or punish the dog with scruff shakes, pinning, or more. A few dogs shut down as a result of this behavior from their owner and the punishment looks successful. However, for most resource-guarding dogs, this kind of correction will increase their guarding. Pinball, and a couple of other extreme resource-guarding dogs I have worked with, have shown me there are elements of anxiety and compulsion to guarding behaviors—both of which would be exacerbated by the above examples of punishment.

☆ More effective remedies for resource guarding involve teaching dogs to happily *drop* anything in their mouths or *leave* things alone on command—initially for treats and then just for praise. When training with treats, many folks forget to also praise their dog, which is essential, as is the timing. If you praise your dog immediately before delivering the treat, the praise becomes conditioned to have the same importance as the treat. Considering Pavlov's bell and our new understanding of neuroplasticity, the rhyme "Neurons that fire together wire together" helps us understand why eventually fading out the treat leaves our praise carrying the same effectiveness.

☆ Sometimes *leave it* and *drop it* are enough, but in the case of a dog like Pinball it can require another couple of levels of training and management. Although his first bite at four months drew no blood, it still qualified as a level two bite on the Dunbar bite scale and identified Pinball as an extreme resource guarder.

» If your voice gets tense or you say, "What do you have?" or "Oh, no, not my expensive such-and-such" with stress or anger in your voice, extreme resource guarders dig in and either run with the object, swallow it, or hold their ground with full display of teeth, growling, and preemptive snapping. Maintaining an attitude of "I don't care; it's all a game" is essential to overcoming this level of resource guarding. One day, I saw Pinball with the pair of scissors in his mouth. "Oh, I hope you're not planning to run like that," I said in a happy tone, and then moved away from him to get my phone to take a picture. I then asked him to *drop it*, returning to him with the treats once he had dropped it. The picture taking is not necessary, but it was a great picture. If I had panicked, he might have bitten me, not dropped the scissors, or tried to swallow them. The "I don't care" rule saved us both that day.

» When originally teaching Pinball to *drop* items, I was using the technique of tossing treats on the floor as I said *drop it* and then picking up the item once he went to get the treats. This has to be done with a happy tone and calm demeanor. Never race the dog to get to the object you want to recover; that could incite the dog to double back.

» For moderate guarders, I recommend building an easy tug game with well-defined boundaries and rules so your dog can learn that letting go of something can be a fun game. Here are simple rules for the tug game:

- Start the game with a word like "*tug*" or "*take it*."

- Keep even pressure on the tug toy so the dog can't move up the toy with her mouth.

- If the dog uses you for leverage with her paws braced against you or her teeth hit you at any point, end the game by dropping the toy and walking away.

- Use only one or two toys to play this game—never use the leash or clothing.

» If you have a resource-guarding dog, please seek out advice from a professional who has dealt with your dog's level of guarding through positive reinforcement and who has an understanding of the emotions involved.

CHAPTER FIVE

Three Birthdays and a Dog Bite

....

The first week in October is Birthday Week—mine is the fifth, Lawrence's is the sixth, and October eighth (the day the adoption was finalized) will be Indy's second birthday each year. Many adoptive families celebrate two birthdays like this for their child every year. It was a couple of weeks later, as Indy turned four month old, that his colic magically ended, as if a switch had been flipped, and he started taking longer naps during the day in addition to sleeping through the night. Life was looking more manageable.

The return to a more routine way of life, however, did not mitigate the toll the dramatic changes to the house had taken on the dogs. Boo, as always, rolled with everything like a good sailor on the high seas, but it was clear he was exhausted, and getting him up the stairs for bedtime was becoming more difficult for him.

Pinball was lost without me available to play with him daily, like before. He was stealing everything that hit the floor. (I thought Indy's first words would be "Pinball, *drop it!*") Realizing he could dig in the backyard while unattended, Pinball did eventually find an appropriate digging spot under a bed of ferns, and when we could not find him outside he was usually asleep in his fern-covered self-made hidey-hole. Pinball had developed a strange relationship with Freya the cat, which continued to escalate. When she would give him a glance, he would fly across the room and pounce on her, as if propelled by some jet engine. Cat-dog mayhem would ensue and when I would take Pinball by the collar to get him off Freya, she would usually sit and wait for me to release Pinball so the unwholesome game could continue.

With all of Pinball's "positive" stressing (in behavioral science, "positive" means "adding to" or taking additional actions), it was hard to see Porthos's negative stressing (meaning he was shutting down and producing fewer actions). Porthos had clearly been internalizing the changes in his life, until it culminated in one of his worst OCD episodes since his massive seizure a year before.

Around the time the colic ended and things were settling down, Porthos started a behavior we knew too well—a type of hacking cough that accompanies obsessive licking at the floor or anything within reach. Lawrence and I had learned to throw everything at this as if it were an attack from outer space, having experienced two similar near bloat episodes in the past. Bloat is an often fatal gastric condition and Porthos's had been so severe it required surgery each time. We knew by now that if we didn't move quickly to stabilize him it would mean another massive surgery, which we swore we wouldn't put him through again. The whole house was put on lockdown. Porthos was watched constantly, muzzled, and given anti-anxiety pills, injectable tranquilizers, and several other medications to keep him, and his gut, as calm as possible. We knew from experience that these attacks could last anywhere from twenty-four hours to a few days.

As a young puppy, Pinball had seen Porthos close to death once before, when he had his worst seizure after one of his surgeries and his blood sugar dropped to 40 (for a diabetic dog like Porthos, a managed blood sugar level is between 70 and 110). Witnessing Porthos's near-death seizure resulted in Pinball developing a hair-trigger reaction to any signs that his buddy might be ill.

Although still trying to monitor Porthos and keep him stable, I had to go out one evening to teach classes. At some point during the evening, he seemed to be seizing and both Lawrence and Pinball went running to his side. Pinball was in high-alert mode, barking and supercharged with vertical energy—he can get some serious height when he is cranked and jumping. There was no way to know what Pinball was saying: it could have been a cry for help, a desire to take advantage of a weaker member of the pack, or even just "Oh my god" over and over in dog. Whatever occurred between Lawrence and Pinball in that moment of panic resulted in Pinball biting Lawrence as Lawrence tried to help Porthos. I wanted to believe that Pinball was trying to guard Porthos, as that is his default mode when stressed (when in doubt—guard it), but in the end I will never know.

Following this episode, it took everything in my power to convince Lawrence that Pinball should not be put down. The bites were fairly deep and not well tended, so they didn't heal quickly, resulting in many days when the evidence of Pinball's crimes were a painful presence. In my efforts to save Pinball's life, I found myself returning to the refrain (for both myself and Lawrence) that Pinball was like a swimming pool: only dangerous when management was not in place, and management had been let go in that instance.

I reminded everyone who interjected on the question of Pinball about one of the greatest therapy dogs I had ever known. The parents were separated and he went with the toddler in the custody swap each week. One weekend at the father's home, the toddler was unrelentingly pestering this usually patient dog. The father did not intervene because he knew this dog to be very good with kids. This dog loved kids so much he would break through his electric fence to go see babies in strollers as they passed by on walks. But on this day he had clearly had enough and bit his toddler badly enough to warrant a trip to the hospital. Afterward, when asked what had happened, the father said, "He's such a good dog, I figured it'd be fine." Ultimately this dog's story was just one of many cautionary tales of the good dog who bites and yet lived happily and safely to the ripe old age of fourteen with the family he loved.

I felt like a broken record, reiterating to family, friends, and myself that no dog can be guaranteed to never bite. There were scores of news articles and family stories about good dogs who bit someone, and at least with Pinball we knew what his issues were and what we had to work on and manage.

It was a hard daily sell to convince Lawrence to keep Pinball, but in the end he agreed to give Pinball another chance. Indy was already recognizing the dogs and had different little sounds for each of them. Whenever Indy saw the mercurial Pinball, he greeted him with a high-pitched giggle, some dolphin-like sounds, and gleeful leg kicks. Pinball was Indy's favorite. It would have been hard on Indy to simply take Pinball out of his life at that point—we had to make this work.

Although Pinball was his favorite, Indy was attached to Boo and Porthos, too. He made an "Ouuuu" sound when he saw Boo—as much as we tried to convince ourselves that Indy was trying to say Boo, that was just not in the four-month-old skill set. One day when I was changing Indy, he started breathing rapidly with his mouth wide open. I was scared to death that he was hyperventilating. As a new parent, many things confounded me, but as a dog trainer I am loath to admit I didn't recognize my baby's attempt to mimic Porthos's happy panting. Given his height, Porthos's head was right at baby level during feeding or story times, and he was the only dog Indy could see from inside the bassinet. As I was trying to decide if I should rush Indy to the doctor, Porthos came up next to the changing table and, as if on cue, began happily panting. Indy panted right back at the big-headed, heavy-breathing dog. I laughed so hard I cried. I think that was probably the most cockeyed diaper Indy has ever worn—it's not easy to diaper a baby squirming to see the panting dog while you can't see through your tears. I now recognized this as Indy's sound for Porthos.

Curiously, although Indy was already expert at telling the difference between the three dogs and the cat, he was still not rolling over. The medical professionals were not concerned, so we focused our worries on dog training and management so Indy could continue to have the animals he already loved in his life.

I juggled the intensified efforts to reinvigorate Pinball's training while keeping Porthos from tipping over into another OCD episode. Luckily, the pharmaceutical cocktail we threw at Porthos's illness held it in check and soon we could just watch him carefully without all the extra medications. The new routine was to keep Porthos in the dining room after meals for about an hour, with the rest of us in the living room. Once we were sure his stomach was settled, we could open the gates and for the rest of the evening all the dogs could hang out with us—as long as I was there.

I had set up a couple of new general rules in the house as well. To start, any time Pinball spent with Indy was only with me right next to them—within inches. Pinball was typically fine lying near me when I fed, changed, or read to Indy. I allowed him to continue to lick Indy's feet and hands gently now that Indy was older and had more immunity, but always ended the sessions early by sliding my hand between Pinball and the baby. These interactions made Indy happy and Pinball seemed to enjoy them, too. My goal was to be sure Pinball loved that little baby as much as he did me so that Pinball would truly think twice before biting my son.

The next rule was that if I was not home, Lawrence, Pinball, and Porthos could not all be in the same room together. They had to have closed gates between them.

Anytime there is a bite or an altercation, we have to look at all the factors involved in the situation. Who was there? What was the environment—inside or outside? If inside, what room were they in? What time of day was it? If we can alter the environment so these factors do not occur again for about a month or more, we have a very good chance of avoiding a dysfunctional pattern of behavior. It is a careful clinical behavior modification approach, and without these restrictions we would run the risk of another bite or altercation. I spent a lot of time worrying that we were not looking at an anomalous bite but instead a new default behavior on Pinball's part, and I wanted to do everything I could to make sure it was not going to become the new norm.

Ironically, just when we could begin to sleep again, I was starting down a long road of sleeplessness. I would dart up suddenly in a panic to check on Porthos if he coughed, and then check the baby monitor to be sure Indy was breathing. Occasionally I found myself downstairs in the kitchen, heart racing, in a panic, holding the insulin. My confusion would include questions such as How did I get there? Did Porthos have his shot? Did I give him another one? Why was I holding the insulin? Was everyone okay? It is an understatement to say these times were stressful, and narcissistic to think I was the only new mother to be panicked by the new levels of stress in her life. I had to assume from the few conversations I heard at Mommy and Me class that each new parent has doubts and obstacles along the way. In some ways I was lucky because my obstacles were in my bailiwick and I had many tools already at my disposal. I had trained the dogs to the point at which their basic skills were reliable. I knew the body language signs to look for from a dog in order to know when it was most likely safe or not safe to interact. I had lived with Porthos's disease for over six years and with the help of a great veterinarian and friend, Julie, we were able to keep him with us.

It can be overwhelming for families who are new to these skills, or families whose dogs develop medical or behavioral issues as they are integrating a new baby into their family. The choices we made to keep Pinball after the bite and Porthos with all his physical ailments were choices that are unique to us. People who have taken dogs into their lives have to make their own decisions, based on their attachment to their dogs, their comfort level in dealing with any issues, and their ability to implement training, behavior modification, and management.

●●●

Training Tips You Can Try at Home

★ Digging

★ Stress

★ Threatening dog body-language cues

★ *Go Sniff* Command

★ Problem dogs and overarching rules for success

★ A dog with a new disease or behavioral issue

★ **Digging** is easy to fix if you can be out in the yard with your dog because conditioning your dog to dig in an appropriate spot will hold over time. However, if you cannot be out with your dog to direct the digging, inappropriate digging will probably continue. Being outside with your dog is the biggest factor when teaching a dog where to dig and where not to dig.

> ☆ If your dog digs, look for a spot where you won't mind a couple of holes. With Dante, our first digger, I gave him a corner next to the deck where nothing grew and I didn't care about a hole or two. Each time he dug in the grassy portion of the yard, I escorted him to the corner next to the deck, where I encouraged him to dig. He caught on quickly and dug only in the corners of the deck for the rest of his life.
>
> With Pinball, we had to fill a few more holes in the grassy area of the yard before he began to reliably dig in more appropriate sections of the backyard because he had more unsupervised time outside. As a result of his being on his own so much, his digging took longer to control.

★ **Stress** in dogs is an exceedingly common occurrence. Often during tests and evaluations, handlers will say, "My dog doesn't get stressed." However, every mammal at some point gets stressed. If we didn't, we wouldn't survive. Stress is a metabolic reaction to external stimuli and a lifesaving mechanism. It can be brought on by a disease that taxes normal bodily functions, a new baby in the home who has changed everyone's sleep patterns, or a tiger jumping out of the trees to eat you. It was first named in 1936 by Dr. Hans Selye to describe the bodily responses he saw in a group of rats he was studying—thus the practice of using what was then an engineering term—"stress"—when referring to certain criteria of metabolic reactions was born.

☆ Useful stress allows us to survive by activating multiple hormones that enhance the function of the heart, lungs, and muscles by increasing heart rate, blood flow, and breathing while slowing or turning off the digestive and immune systems. Those reactions help us escape from something dangerous by running (flight), engaging (fight), or hiding (freezing).

☆ Chronic stress is not useful because it keeps the automatic, sympathetic, and parasympathetic nervous systems in a constant state of alert, just as a car left running when it's parked will eventually run out of gas and wear out the battery.

☆ Both people and dogs can have physical and behavioral responses to stress, especially chronic stress.

» Physical stress for dogs or people can lead to sleeplessness and weight fluctuation, either gain or loss. It can also fuel a variety of diseases or make current diseases worse.

TRAINING TIPS

» When people get stressed, they can have a shorter fuse and be quick to anger, often can't focus, and might be constantly on high alert.

» When dogs get stressed, they frequently can't follow simple commands (can't focus), and they are quicker to bark and lunge at a given trigger (shorter fuse and/or higher alert mode).

» Like people, dogs will try to regulate the stress in their environment, and we can see those efforts in their body language. (For more information, see Chapter Two or the section below on body language.)

- Dogs will offer any of the calming signals I spoke about in Chapter Two, along with others listed below and some that are specific to an individual dog. I can name each of my dog's default stress responses: Boo paces, Porthos shuts down and then licks and eats indigestible items, and Pinball steals things. It is important that parents can predict what their dogs will do when stressed so they can be aware of it when it happens.

- Stressed dogs will often be less reliable on their basic commands. I see this sign of stress in testing situations when the handler, unaware of the dog's stress, inevitably says, "But my dog does this behavior at home."

- I reply, "But you're not at home and the stress here is very different."

- If your dog is too stressed, worried, or excited around your baby, the dog's basic behaviors may falter.

★ Dogs give us some very specific, threatening, body language cues. If calming signals are a level yellow threat, the body language signals below are more threatening levels—orange or even red—and therefore indicate a need to get your dog out of the situation immediately.

☆ Ears are big indicators. The natural state of your dog's ears is important to recognize and will be different for each dog depending on their breed, personality, and their own personal development. For example, not all German Shepherds have ears that stand straight up in the air. Some are bent or a little flopped over. Some dogs have cropped ears and others have variations on folded and flopped. Regardless, each dog has a natural neutral ear position, which tells us that he is engaging with us in a neutral way—maybe a little happy, maybe disinterested, but not fearful.

» If the ears perk up, it indicates a dog who is actively engaging in something and it might be exciting, fun, or troubling. If the ears are up, the dog is on alert.

» Flattened ears (when a dog pins his ears back against his head) indicate the dog is worried or afraid and probably thinks he needs to protect himself, especially if he is being approached, petted, or worse—hugged!

☆ A dog bracing her back legs way behind her as if she is getting ready to bolt at any minute is scared or at least conflicted. We often see this when a dog is sniffing someone or something she is unsure about. She will probably not be okay with being petted or grabbed by little baby hands at this point. It is best to get the dog out of the situation and then see if she wants to return to investigate again with less stress—or take a break from the situation completely.

☆ These signals can easily be missed if we don't know what we are seeing and can result in a situation in which someone says, "That dog bit my child and there was no warning." The warning could have been something along these lines: The dog approached with braced back legs (Warning #1) and then looked away (Warning #2) and followed that

TRAINING TIPS

with a whale eye (Warning #3). The progression of these three warnings tell us the problem was not being defused and was getting worse. The dog then became still or stiff (Warning #4) and then flattened his ears (Warning #5). These last two warnings would be the equivalent of the dog saying, "Step away, or I'll bite." Although most owners would have only seen the whale eye, there were four other warning signals here that are often missed because they come in quick succession and can be subtle. I often see dogs desperately asking for help using some of the signals above, and when they do, we need to step in and stop whatever interaction is occurring.

★ The *go sniff* command allows you to help your dog exit a stressful situation, or get out of Dodge. The ***go sniff*** command tells your dog to "go over there" (choose an area away from the trigger) and start looking for treats. We usually start teaching this behavior when your dog is not stressed by tossing some treats as you say, "*Go sniff.*" Your dog happily follows the treats and then has to look for them. When you use this in a stressful situation it lets you move the dog out of harm's way and keeps him busy for a minute or more, while you figure out what to do next—move baby, close gate, and so on. Because this command is one of the easiest to teach and learn, is an innate behavior (chasing things that move—especially food), and almost always has a treat involved in its execution, it is one of the few commands that usually works even when a dog is stressed and over threshold.

★ For problem dogs, I have a couple of overarching rules.
My first rule for problem dogs is the No Panic Rule. If we go into panic mode when our dog does something we don't like or think is

potentially dangerous, it often makes matters worse. Swift action is essential, but action with a composed and even playful air will keep your dog from responding to your panic with his own panic—like swallowing the stolen object, barking louder, jumping higher, running away in fear, or biting. Remaining calm and even silly in the face of something scary is easier said than done, but with some conscious thought and practice it is definitely possible. As with so much about raising a child, once we practice being calm and patient with our dogs while keeping management in place, it becomes another element in our regular routine like changing a diaper, feeding the baby, and general daily tasks.

My second rule comes in the form of a rhyme: "When in doubt, get the dog out." Because we want our dog to be our baby's buddy and learn how to get along with strangers or other dogs, we often force the dog into situations she is not ready to face. We need to let our dog process a new or scary thing at her own pace. This often means having to do something that may seem counterintuitive—let her *go sniff* in another room or several feet away from the crying baby or the unknown relative who just arrived. You might think if the dog is not right next to the baby, she won't get used to him or her, or if she is not getting petted by our relatives or friends, she won't get used to them. It's important to remember some dogs need time to hear or view the baby or visitor from a distance before they can come close for commands, treats, or pets. Once the dog has some distance, she can process the stressor more easily and begin to adjust to it. Your dog will tell you what she needs, but you have to be ready to listen to what she tells you so you can help her. We have to remember the final behavior we are trying to achieve will usually not be built in a day.

Sometimes we will ask the dog to go into the bedroom for solitary playtime when things are too scary or too complicated. This

TRAINING TIPS

downtime allows the dog to avoid making stress-related mistakes and live to see another day so we can slowly expose her to more people and more sights and sounds when she is more comfortable. The goal is that she will be able to participate a little more over time.

Michelangelo said, "Every block of stone has a statue inside it and it is the task of the sculptor to discover it." This is as much about dog training and child rearing as it is sculpting. Every day we work with our dog and our child to help them get along happily and safely, we are sculpting the Timmy and Lassie image we all have of dogs and kids in our heads. I would rather work at a slow pace and be sure everyone is safe and happy than push things too quickly and find out I have a problem that could cost the life of my dog, injure my child, or send me back to the beginning of my behavioral modification work.

★ **A dog with a new disease or behavioral issue** will require additional work and attention. It is best to address this issue as soon as it appears and work out a plan. It is essential you talk to your veterinarian so he or she can work closely with you. Your veterinarian will need to know your time may be short because of the new baby and you may need to speak to them at odd hours. I am lucky that Porthos had Dr. Julie, who listened closely to my descriptions of his ailments and worked with me to stabilize him each time there was an issue. If you don't feel you can talk to your veterinarian when there are issues, then get a second opinion. Support from your veterinarian, and trainer, could make all the difference in the world.

CHAPTER SIX

Reflections After the Storm

....

October continued to be a tricky month. I was still waking most nights to run through my checklist to be sure Porthos was okay, check Indy, and occasionally calm Pinball if Porthos coughed or made any strange vocalization. I really wanted to hunker down and do nothing until I knew everyone was back on an even keel for a couple of months, but a conference and book signing in Cincinnati took me away from all my boys (human and canine) for almost a week.

I reminded Lawrence of the new rules put into place after the bite and added some extra management elements before I left. First, in addition to not having Porthos and Pinball in the same room when I was not home, we would return to using Pinball's corral whenever Porthos was in the living room, Lawrence was in doubt when things got a little hectic, or food was in play. The corral is one of the highest levels of management. It is a crate with a few sides of a play yard attached to it to make a slightly larger area—like building an addition on a crate. This was even more of a limitation on Pinball's freedom than we had initially implemented when Indy first came home. Normal management did not require the dogs being crated, but after Pinball's infraction, he was on house arrest. Luckily, it was an easy increase above standard management because we had the corral in place when Pinball was a puppy and he was already comfortable in it.

Second, getting Pinball into his corral or another room meant Lawrence had to employ new methods. Normally, he would guide each dog by his collar to wherever he wanted him. But I wanted no hands on Pinball, so I taught Lawrence the *touch* command to move Pinball with hand gestures and the *go sniff* command. Pinball already knew them with me and, although he loved them, he still needed rewards to comply with them.

These commands did two things—they allowed Lawrence to remain at a safe distance from Pinball as they rebuilt their relationship, and allowed Pinball to start viewing Lawrence not as "the guy who's gonna grab me" but as "the guy with the treats in the other room." If the *touch* command didn't work, Lawrence would fall back to *go sniff* or, as a last resort, he could try *luring*, which Lawrence and Pinball both already knew well.

The downside to *luring* was that it didn't offer the distance between Pinball and Lawrence that *touch* and *go sniff* did, but I wanted Lawrence to have multiple options because Pinball and Lawrence vexed each other. Pinball is a dog seemingly designed to exasperate humans. Lawrence would give a command, and Pinball wouldn't respond. Lawrence would repeat the command, Pinball would refuse again, and back and forth it would go. So I taught Lawrence my second rule for problem dogs. When Pinball pushed all his buttons to the breaking point, Lawrence was to remember this mantra, "When in doubt, get him out." By the time I left for the conference, Lawrence could move Pinball anywhere—into the corral, into another room in the house, or outside and back inside—without touching or getting annoyed with him. *Touch*, *go sniff*, and *luring* are great techniques for any home with a baby and dogs because it allows the parent to move the dogs away from the baby with simple cues that make everyone happy.

The Association of Professional Dog Trainers (APDT) conference is always mentally exhausting. By the end the entire conference is an intellectual blur, going from a workshop on behavior to a lecture on training to a demonstration of technique and round and round for five days straight. That year, I saw Pinball in every session. In the workshops on aggressive dogs, I had to wonder, were they talking about Pinball? Was the lecture on resource guarding going to help or hurt Pinball? Well, at least the lecture on tug was perfectly in line with Pinball's and my love of the game. When I wasn't paranoid the speakers were talking directly to me about Pinball, I worried that some catastrophe was unfolding at home, waiting to greet me upon my return. But the universe had another disaster in store for me. My elderly mother had taken a downturn in her battle with Alzheimer's disease and kidney failure. My sister did not expect her to last the week, so I took a day trip to Chicago from the conference to say goodbye as my mother was moved into hospice.

Just as I was thinking this was more than enough stress for one month and October couldn't get any worse, Superstorm Sandy arrived a week after I got back from the conference. Like so many in this hurricane, we lost power and, after scouring the land for the last generator in Putnam County, did our best to ride it out. With our emergency generator, we were only able to run the refrigerator, the microwave, and some lamps. But as the temperatures started to drop, it simply wasn't safe to keep a four-month-old baby in a home with no heat, no running water—hot or cold—and only the fireplace to keep all of us warm.

Indy weathered the storm better than the dogs. He was happy to be hanging out with all of us in our twenty-by-twenty living room made cozy by the constant fires, but the dogs were already stressed by the sound of the storm and the following confusion. It was difficult to navigate the house with the few lights the generator could power and there was no light at all in the yard at night. When power goes out we humans miss all the amenities, but the dogs notice things on a different level. Without electricity, our homes lose their regular hum and many dogs are sensitive to this. I have clients whose dogs with thunderstorm phobia also develop lack-of-power phobia because dogs (like humans) make connections between events that happen together. It's a kind of conditioned superstitious behavior that tells them when the house doesn't hum, there's probably thunder on the way—therefore no power is as scary as thunder.

By day seven, Indy's aunties had their power restored. He and I went to stay there while Lawrence tried to prevent the pipes from freezing by keeping fires going in the fireplace, as he looked after the confused and stressed animals.

After ten days our power was restored and we were all back together with a collective feeling of "What else could go wrong?" Unsurprisingly, the universe had one last item on the agenda for us. A day after our power returned, I was off on another plane to Chicago for my mother's funeral. By this time, Lawrence knew the new rules well and, as I left, I had the comfort of feeling a little less fearful that a report of a dog calamity would await my return.

I had hoped to fly out the morning of the funeral and fly back that night. My sister and I had never been close, so I knew I would not be welcome for longer than the funeral. I had watched the weather before leaving—they predicted snow, but no hurricanes—and made a preemptive reservation at a Chicago airport hotel. As I had anticipated, I was stranded in the airport hotel and had time to reflect on how I was doing setting up the dogs and Indy for success.

As it turned out, my ability to do all the things I had wanted to as far as training, desensitizing and counter-conditioning, and building calm, happy, quality time had been eroded by real life. Struggling to jam training into the small gaps of time between running my business, taking care of the baby, and promoting my book was tricky. But adding in major events like Porthos's OCD episode, Superstorm Sandy, and my mother's passing truly gummed up the works. Instead of training, I was relying more on management, like the baby gates, and separation than I had originally wanted to. At least that allowed for some desensitization to happen while giving the dogs some space from each other and time to process all the new elements in their lives.

My hope was that by this point I would have been more at ease with the dogs hanging out with Indy, so they could all be in the room for his belly time and initial crawling. As it was, each dog was at a different stage. During belly time, Boo was allowed to roam freely in the room, Porthos was allowed to be on his pillow or up on the bed, but Pinball needed to be in a hard *settle* with me between them both. There was still no way for them all to be together for belly time. The progress I had made was so far from perfect, the distance could be measured in light years. But Boo had taught me, through our journey together, that patience is the most powerful training tool and perfect is not all it's cracked up to be. I had to view it as ongoing success, and at least we were making progress toward our goal. It also made me acknowledge that perhaps my goals were not realistic with the collection of animals we had. I also realized, if I had unrealistic goals as a professional, what could I expect from the average pet owners' goals for their babies and dogs?

It became clear that the biggest issue surrounding dogs being rehomed (or worse) when a new baby arrives are the unrealistic expectations parents have for their dogs. Many pet owners seem to overestimate their dog's ability to roll with the changes in the household and accept the new threats the baby poses—and it's not always the first baby. One of my clients contacted me about trying to save her neighbor's small twelve-year-old terrier mix from euthanasia when the dog growled at one of the neighbor's children. In response, the family wanted the dog out of their house immediately. This dog had lived with the family all of her life and with the two-year-old, four-year-old, and seven-year-old children for all of theirs. I explained that at twelve years old it would be hard for this dog to be adopted and suggested she should be checked for a newly developed disease. Conditions such as arthritis can cause dogs to be cranky and less patient with three young children doing normal kid things. The fact that the family chose to euthanize their dog after one growl reinforces for me that too many pet owners have extraordinarily high expectations for their dogs that are often not realistic for many pets. A dog who growls allows us to take care of things before they get out of control, and taking care of our dog always helps us take care of our children. I had to wonder how those kids would process their dog's demise and if it might have a lasting impression on them.

I knew how much the dogs were already a part of Indy's life, and how much they helped me keep him happy. That was probably the biggest positive in all our canine chaos up to this point—our ability to keep Indy happy. It was always possible to make him laugh. Either the sight of Pinball made him giddy with laughter, or Porthos's crazy panting made him grin and pant back, or farting noises or belly raspberries would reliably crack him up. My goal was to keep him as happy as possible, no matter how antithetical to the situation it seemed. I knew from my work with fearful dogs that so much of their sensitivity and anxiety hinges on their early development. I had also learned from so many seminars and webinars that the chemical makeup of our own human brains can be set up for happiness or depression very early in life. Not just nature, but nurture plays a big role. In spite of the pummeling of sad, depressing, and generally hard emotions we were all experiencing at this time, we pulled together to keep the baby laughing.

• • •

Training Tips You Can Try at Home

* ★ Levels of management
* ★ The *touch* command
* ★ *Luring*
* ★ Emergency preparedness

★ Levels of management can be broken down into five main categories in our house. Your home may need more or fewer depending on you, your baby, and your dog.

☆ Having your dog in a completely separate room from your guests or your baby with a locked door is the highest level of management. Although it provides the most security for everyone and allows your dog to still hear and smell the guests or the baby, it is limited in terms of helping her adjust to these new elements in her life. However, if your goal is to have her away from guests who don't like dogs or are allergic, then behind the locked door is perfect. Be sure your dog has a puzzle toy with great snacks while she is sequestered.

☆ A crate is the second-highest level of management for your dog. I prefer a standard wire dog crate located so your dog is securely away from everyone and everything. Two-door crates offer more placement options because of doors on two sides. Wire crates allow the dog maximum airflow and the ability to observe what's going on outside the crate. Also, you can see or reward the dog through the wires. The crate should not be located in the middle of a thoroughfare or the center of hubbub in the home. It is nice to have the crate off to the side of a room where the family generally relaxes, like family rooms or bedrooms. There are some nice crate tables available that allow the crate to be disguised as a piece of furniture. Or if you're handy, you can do what I did and build a "lid" so it acts like a table. Regardless of what room the crate goes into, it should be in a heated and air-conditioned room away from any appliances that make noises.

☆ The corral and/or play yard is the third level of management. To construct the corral, I take a few panels from a plastic play yard and attach them to the corners of a two-door crate so one of the doors is enclosed by the play yard. This can be done with a single-door crate if your dog is small and does not mind being physically put in the crate—however, I like to avoid physically putting any dog into a crate (big or small). With a two-door crate, your dog can enter on her own through one door and then go out the second door to get into the corral area. This gives her more room than the crate alone and allows you and others more access to her over the sides of the play yard. The crate still provides an area where she can retreat in order to feel safe from anyone reaching in—such as kids or guests. Both doors of the crate can be closed so she is completely contained in the crate.

Using a play yard set up as a freestanding corral works almost as well as a crate-corral, except the dog has no area that is unreachable, so it doesn't offer the same level of safety from or for reaching hands.

☆ Having your dog behind a baby gate is the fourth level of management. That allows her to be in an adjacent room without free access to you, your baby, or your guests, while people can reach over and through the spindles to deliver treats and petting if both parties are interested. However, the dog can jump up on the gates, which most of us don't want. Ideally, all interactions with the dog at the gate need to be with her either sitting or standing, but not jumping, lest that behavior becomes reinforced. This level of management is ideal for your dog to see new people and have treats tossed to her so she begins to get used to and be happy about seeing people.

It is important to be careful if your dog is afraid of approaching strangers or toddlers because allowing folks to approach a fearful dog before the dog is ready could increase her fears. The baby gates could leave the guests or your baby vulnerable if your dog feels cornered.

☆ Within short reach is the lowest level of management, meaning you are within reaching distance of both your dog and your baby. Perhaps the baby is having belly time and your dog is in a settle with you between her and the baby. Or maybe you are reading to your baby on your lap with your dog sitting next to you, sniffing the baby's feet. This level of management is only possible if your dog has reliable *sit*, *stay*, *settle*, and *go sniff* commands so you can easily instruct her during these interactions. It is also necessary that your dog be interested in this interaction—not forced there. If we force our dog into close proximity with our baby when she is not happy being there, we will not be developing a positive association or relationship between her and our child.

★ The *touch* **command** is one of the most versatile foundational skills, on which we can build a host of other, more complicated commands. For the purposes of guiding a dog around a baby, the *touch* command allows us to use our hand to position the dog without having to grab her.

☆ To teach it, start with a flat hand and place a treat between your thumb and palm. Swipe your hand as in a magician's ta-da gesture in front of your dog's nose, letting her catch the scent of the treat, then say "*touch*," and, as if you are doing a bow or curtsy, continue the swipe of your hand away from her a few feet. Your dog will usually follow the moving hand to get to the treat. Reward her with the treat when her nose touches your hand. After a couple of repetitions, fade the food from your swiping hand while you ask for the *touch*, but keep rewarding from the other hand.

☆ You can follow this by tossing the treat even farther away from you so you can move the dog through a gate, out a door, or away from anything. Usually I will give the *go sniff* command if I do the extra tossing of the treat so these two gestures become two different commands—*touch* means "nose to the hand" and *go sniff* means "move farther away."

★ *Luring* is often misunderstood, but it is invaluable. To *lure* we have a treat or toy in our hands and use it like a magnet to attract the dog (the piece of metal). We can *lure* our dog into positions like a *sit* or *down* or into a crate or another room. We give the dog the treat or toy we were using as the *lure* once he complies. The downside to *luring* is that if we are not careful and don't fade the *lure* from our hand relatively quickly, it will always have to be there. The trick is to give a verbal command before initiating the *lure* sequence so the command is what the dog will respond to and the *lure* can be easily faded. (More on *luring* in Chapter Eleven.)

★ **Emergency preparedness** can be difficult to plan when there are so many individuals to take care of, some of whom are not welcome in various shelter settings.

Some standard things to consider when taking care of a small child or animals during a power outage are heat, cooking capacity, fresh water, and refrigeration (Porthos's insulin had to be refrigerated). A generator, even a small one, will allow you to have at least some of these.

Without access to those necessities, most folks will go either to a hotel if the emergency is not widespread or to a shelter if money or widespread outages make a hotel an impossibility.

Many hotels and shelters do not accept the family pet(s). Lawrence and I have never taken advantage of shelters or hotels in the numerous outages we have had over the years because we won't leave our animals.

I would urge families with animals and children and no generator to have a list of options that will allow them to take care of the whole family—hopefully together.

☆ Locate the nearest family shelters and hotels that accept pets. Be sure to check on restrictions based on your pet's size or number of pets. Have the numbers handy and make reservations as soon as the storm is predicted.

☆ Have a list of friends and relatives who can take you and your pets if their home has power and is not flooded or damaged. Remember to ask them ahead of time; don't assume.

☆ Some folks like a go-bag. I don't usually put one together since the things in it might expire by the time I would use it. Instead, I keep all emergency supplies and equipment in the same cabinet so I can easily access what I need or throw it into a bag.

» Dry baby formula or breast pump, many bottles, diapers and diapering supplies, along with multiple changes of clothing for the baby (and you, too—let's face it, a messy poop can get everywhere), and a few favorite toys to occupy the baby.

» Pet food and medications, feeding and water bowls—one for each pet.

» Leashes, harnesses, and collars. Be sure they fit ahead of time. Depending on your pet, you may also need towels and blankets.

» ID tags with phone numbers, rabies tags, and the rabies certificate. One easy thing to do is make a copy of your pet's rabies certificate as soon as the vet gives it to you and keep it in the glove compartment of your car. This will come in handy if your dog ever gets lost or picked up by animal control.

☆ You may want a crate for your dog for a number of reasons. If your dog is small, it will be easier for you, but with bigger dogs that are not friendly to strangers or other dogs, a crate will allow for safe, movable containment. Be sure to think about this ahead of time and ask shelters about crate requirements or restrictions.

» If you cannot all stay together, have a list of boarding facilities in and out of your area in case you must board your pets for the short- or long-term.

☆ If you decide to stay home, you will still need a list of items to have at the ready.

TRAINING TIPS

» A generator (regularly tested) can often allow everyone
to stay home when there is no flooding, fire, or home
destruction.

» Find the safest spot in the home and be sure everyone fits—
or have a couple of spots that will be safe and accommodate
everyone.

» Just as you would keep yourself and your children inside,
please keep your pets inside—even if it means cleaning up
some pee or poop when the storm passes. One of our neighbors was killed horribly in her driveway when walking her dog
during the Halloween storm of 2011. If the weather-person
says don't go out, don't—not even for a quick pee.

» If your pets become skittish at wind or thunder and try to
run out of the house if the door opens, please have them on
leash or in a crate.

☆ After the storm—regardless of whether you evacuated or
stayed home—remember the landscape and the home, if
damaged, will be different and confusing for many pets.
Please keep them on leash when outside, and inside if the
home has openings due to damage, until things are repaired.

CHAPTER SEVEN

Still Plagued by the Bite, and He Drops FOOD!

....

I t isn't long after babies begin to eat their first solid food that most dogs discover this little human-like creature drops food—and from the dog's perspective it's super-high-value food! Some parents discourage their dog from eating these morsels, but I wanted my dogs to associate Indy with all good things. So when there were droppings on the floor, I would let the boys clean up (provided the food was safe for dogs to eat). In the beginning there wasn't much, but it was enough to make the dogs view Indy in a whole new light.

As Indy began to sample food with his formula at mealtime, we started with bananas, which he loved as much as the dogs did. We then introduced peas and chicken, sweet potatoes, peaches, and pears. In short, there wasn't anything Indy didn't eat and there wasn't anything he ate that the dogs didn't love, too. Given Porthos's diabetes, I was careful about what I let him scarf up. I also reduced both his and Pinball's regular food intake depending on what they got from the floor.

Pinball and Porthos began eagerly arranging themselves beneath the high chair at mealtimes for the Indy slot machine. But Boo still had not figured out that the baby was paying off like a projectile one-armed bandit, and I left it that way, given the complexity of it all. It was becoming harder and harder for Boo to find his own bowl when we directed him to it, so letting him try to vie for any of the dropped food was bound to lead to altercations as he bumped into the other dogs while searching blindly. As it was, I knew that I was taking a risk letting Porthos and Pinball engage in this behavior because they both had resource-guarding issues. Pinball was a Bond-esque super-villain of resource guarding, while Porthos was more like a street-thug guarding amateur. His guarding was only directed at other dogs when he wasn't feeling well. Given that my primary mission with this activity was to establish Indy as a very good thing to have around from the dogs' point of view, I was willing to take the chance and see how it went. I set them up in specific spots using the *settle* command and monitored them closely, knowing that I might have to put a stop to it at any moment.

And it worked! Indy was now almost as important to them as I was. He was not just a curiosity—he was valuable to them. But as suspected, there was behavioral fallout. One meal I saw a hard stare and whale eye shoot between Porthos and Pinball, and I knew the open grazing at the baby's chair was all over. From then on, one would have breakfast, and the other dinner. This new schedule was easy to accomplish with the gates and each dog's solid *touch* and *stay* commands. Like a traffic cop, I could direct one to hold position, ask the other to come forward past the gate for *touch*—and then release the one in the *stay* after I closed the gate.

Things seemed to be going well with the separate slot machine times until one night when Pinball was having his turn with Indy. He was lying under the high chair when Lawrence bent to pick up something unidentifiable nearby (not food or a toy) and Pinball air-snapped in Lawrence's direction. An air snap is a warning—no teeth hit anyone, but it has to be taken seriously. Pinball lost his slot machine privileges after that and so did Porthos. Keeping it the same for all dogs was the best way to be sure the rules would be consistently followed. Clearly, the bonding attempt had been powerful. It turned out Pinball was actually guarding the whole setup: Indy, the chair, and everything in the vicinity. Resource-guarding super-villain indeed.

In our house the downside to letting the dogs learn the baby was a slot machine were significant, but for a time they were outweighed by the upside of the incredible positive association the dogs built with Indy. Throughout my career I have kept myself safe and out of the mouths of biting dogs by making sure they knew I was a vending machine that would toss out treats if the dogs hit the right buttons with their behavior. One dog, whose final bite resulted in twenty-three stitches for a volunteer at the shelter, never bit me to his dying day. I knew it was only because his affection for me (and my safety) was bought with treats. Armed with the knowledge of what a powerful protective association treating a dog can produce, I thought it was worth taking a chance to build that connection for Pinball and Porthos with Indy.

In general there are other downsides beyond the guarding we saw that could be born of the baby-drops-things game. Some dogs might start to get grabby with their mouths (many dogs exhibit harder mouths—chomping down to get treats, toys, and so on—when they are excited or stressed), they might start to demand-bark if the dropped food is not coming quickly enough, or they might begin physically pushing for more (pawing at the baby, nudging with their nose, or nibbling at the baby). Given the downsides to this interaction, it has to be thoroughly thought through with constant oversight and with a back-out plan in place, or it could result in an inadvertent injury to the parent or child. Even the simple act of letting the dog clean up after a baby who tosses a good portion of his or her food has to be monitored and managed so it doesn't become trouble. For example, if a dog begins to guard the spot where the food has fallen—as Pinball did—then this technique might not be helping. In the end, you have to weigh the pros and cons of this positive association technique based on the dogs you have and your household.

Even though the baby casino had closed down for the dogs, I continued to let Indy spend time with each of them in other situations, with close supervision, especially for Pinball. Indy was now five months old and even though we were still waiting for him to roll over, there was no delay in his affection for that crazy dog. Indy refused to be carried like other babies—upright on the hip. Instead, he insisted on being carried like a football—essentially flying through the air headfirst. That was how I instruct clients to hold puppies, so it made perfect sense to me. Riding like this allowed Indy to see the dogs perfectly as he hovered above their heads. As soon as I would turn Indy over for transport, he would kick his legs and squeal in delight as he watched Pinball run past in a furry blur. There was no denying that Pinball—the wild card—made Indy laugh, giggle, and smile like no other human or other animal.

Based on the unusual deference Pinball showed Indy, the feelings seemed mutual. Pinball's height made it difficult for him to see Indy face-to-face most of the time, but Indy was the one person Pinball didn't jump on—even when he was easily accessible as he flew by in football position. And Pinball wanted to be wherever Indy was. When it was time to get Indy up, change him, take him back up for naptime, or feed him, Pinball was always there. In short, Indy didn't go anywhere without Pinball trailing along, unless I shut the door as I did for bath time. Eventually I got tired of seeing Pinball's shadow under the door as he hovered patiently outside the bathroom. So I compromised, and Pinball was allowed into bath time if he *settled* on the pillow in the bathroom. It wasn't long before Indy was pitching his toys from the tub to the dog on the pillow. I was starting to understand they were equally matched in their troublemaking skills, but at least we got to practice Pinball's *leave its* and *drop its* during bath time.

I was determined to make this Pinball thing work, not only because of my desire to let Indy have the dog he loved in his life, but also because of my own personal attachment to Pinball. Being at the shelter the day Pinball was born, and then nursing him through parvovirus, left me feeling a deep responsibility for him. I wanted to help him be the happy-go-lucky safe dog that he was when he was a puppy. I focused on making sure everyone in the household could be in compliance with management rules at all times, and that there were treat containers in every room where Pinball would be: the kitchen, the living room, the nursery, my bathroom, and the master bedroom. I also spent time working on the reliability of Pinball's stationary commands in the face of a stressor like Porthos, dropped toys, or proximity to the baby. The other point we had to focus on was making sure Lawrence and I were on the same page with the resource-guarding behavior modification. Owners with resource-guarding dogs often feel the dogs are "getting away" with something when they pay their dog to release an object. To some extent they are, but we are the smart humans and have the ability to tweak the behavior so eventually the dogs are not getting away with anything and we are all getting what we need. It comes down to accepting where the dog is as a baseline, rewarding for that baseline behavior, and then slowly asking for a little more, and a little more.

Establishing a training plan is the first step, but management and consistency have to be applied for the plan to work. In theory, management and consistency offer big behavioral changes and are easy, but the reality is they can be the hardest parts of the plan to implement. The enemies of management are behaviors such as "I forgot to shut the gate," or "The dog was too fast," or "I didn't realize where the dog was." The enemy of consistency, in contrast, comes in the form of "What were we supposed to do? I didn't remember." Implementation of a training plan requires the family to adopt new behaviors and execute them without fail in a situation that is already complicated by life changes, lack of sleep, and usually a to-do list that doesn't seem to end. All families trying to keep their babies and dogs safe together need to keep in mind training is a process that has to be considered every day. With daily attention, it will soon become second nature. The dog-baby relationship is like the child-parent relationship, in that they are both relationships that require us to build and rebuild as we go, but if we put in the work it will hopefully last for the long haul.

• • •

Training Tips You Can Try at Home:

★ Human foods
★ Baby-leftovers
★ Resource guarding
★ Showing baby how to pet the dog gently

★ **Human foods** like hot dogs, cheese, or leftover chicken can be used for treats or placed in a puzzle toy when guests come over. They are not necessarily bad for dogs, and do not encourage them to beg (unless you feed them from your plate or table). However, there are foods that dogs should not eat. Keep your veterinarian's and pet poison control hotline's numbers where you can easily find them in an emergency.

☆ Some of the foods that are <u>highly toxic and potentially fatal</u> for your dog are chocolate, coffee (really all caffeine), grapes, raisins, avocados, and xylitol.

☆ Some of the foods that <u>should be avoided</u> are onions, garlic, chives, and macadamia nuts.

These are just a sampling of foods that should not be given to your dog. The ASPCA has a longer list on their website. They also have a twenty-four-hour helpline that charges a fee, but having used that service twice—once for Porthos and once for Pinball—I can tell you it was well worth it.

★ **Baby leftovers** is a game that builds a powerful positive association between baby and dog but presents dangers and pitfalls. As evidenced by Pinball's issues, this game is usually not a good idea for dogs who are resource guarders, and it is also not ideal for dogs who have a history of demand barking, pawing, or nibbling.

☆ The baby-leftovers game sometimes goes on inadvertently and sometimes intentionally for reasons like these: "It's easier for the dog to clean up the crumbs on the floor," or "I didn't notice the dog lying under the high chair was really eating everything that fell."

☆ If you wish to implement this game to build a stronger bond between your baby and dog(s), or you are letting it go on because there seems to be no harm, it is imperative that you are able to interpret your dog's body language instantly and accurately. If you miss the low stare with whale eye from your dog under the high chair and your child reaches down to pet her in that moment, it could result in a growl, snap, or bite.

☆ This game has huge potential to strengthen a bond or to backfire if you are not well versed in resource guarding, demand behavior, or dog body language. When in doubt regarding this game, reach out to a trainer with extensive successful positive reinforcement experience in resource guarding and dog body language.

☆ For other dogs with no resource issues, this game helps parents clean up and further bonds your dog to the tiny projectile slot machine that is your baby.

★ **Resource guarding** in dogs has several books devoted to it alone. Here I will cover more of the detailed techniques we used with Pinball's extreme guarding, which can be applied to any resource-guarding dog, but folks whose dog has resource-guarding issues on Pinball's level should seek out an experienced trainer (see Chapter Eight for advice on choosing a trainer).

Resource guarding sometimes begins as a game for puppies and then morphs into a state of worry, panic, or anxiety because they fear they are going to lose their toy or food. Understanding it can have an anxiety component, not unlike human hoarders, allows us to see why taking the object away forcibly most often increases the guarding and any aggressive response to us.

The notion that the dog is getting away with something only puts us in an adversarial position with our dog, when what we need to do is retool our dog's emotional relationship with the object and us.

☆ When I began working with Pinball's resource guarding at four months, I would say, "*Drop it*" and then lay out a string of treats almost four feet long. I had to step back from the end of the string before he would comfortably leave the object to eat the treats. I knew he would bolt back to the object if I raced him to it and he would likely bite me. To avoid that, when he got to the end of the string of treats, I tossed a few more treats away with a *go sniff* command so he would move even farther from the object. Only then could I safely pick up the object.

☆ After I knew what process would safely allow me to take the object, that process became the baseline from which we worked. It was tedious, but regularly saying *drop it* before I laid out the treats taught Pinball that *drop it* meant he was going to get something good. Soon the length of the string of treats could be shortened and the quantity of treats could be dialed back for most objects. There were still a few objects, like baby blocks, that required more treats to buy them back from Pinball. When he started offering a signal—circling once or twice on his pillow before lying down in *settle* position (very different from his "I want to keep this" hover)—I knew it meant he would drop the object and I could safely remove it for praise and treats.

☆ This routine was the norm for a long time. But eventually after I praised him, I added in a trick before the treats so I could build a chain of behaviors. The chain became *drop it*, he circled and lay down on the pillow, and he dropped the toy. I then praised him, asked for his apologize trick (which meant he would stretch his chin out and rest it on his front paws), praised him again, and then I treated him while I picked up the toy.

☆ It took another several months before I could pick up the toy before delivering the treat with all the chained behavior in place. It was another several months after that before I could take low-value objects from him with praise but no treats.

☆ I will always have to pay Pinball for high-value objects or when stressors are elevated in the house. We are, however, claiming a victory because in most cases we have changed his emotional state regarding the loss of his resources and we can read via his body language if that emotional change has not occurred. Then we employ the rules we have developed to keep us all safe.

★ **Showing your baby how to pet the dog gently** is as important as teaching your dog to be happy about your baby. Younger children will not have enough motor control to pet your dog gently. Consequently, many dogs get hit, pulled, poked, or a combination of all of these instead of the snuggly petting they are used to from adults.

TRAINING TIPS

☆ When a young child is petting a dog, an adult needs to be next to and almost between the dog and child in order to guide the child's hand as he or she tries to pet the dog. I usually keep my hand at or hovering just under Indy's hand so I can slip my hand between him and Boo instantly if things go wrong.

Petting a dog is a great motor skills exercise for toddlers, but it is not something they can master until they develop more. Be prepared to be attentive to this petting for a couple of years until you see your child has the appropriate motor control and skills.

» I encourage young children to pet dogs on the side of the body, avoiding the top of the head, tail, or even the chest area in the beginning. These areas are sensitive for dogs and to reach them the child often has to be right in front of the dog's mouth.

» Think of this slow introduction to dog petting like using training wheels on a bicycle. As your child gets better and demonstrates an understanding of the concepts, you will slowly introduce more petting of different dog body parts. But expecting young children to be able to pet their dog appropriately on their own could lead to the dog becoming fearful of the little baby pincers (fingers) and the child being injured.

TRAINING TIPS

CHAPTER EIGHT

Everyone Has Opinions—Fingers in Your Ears

···

What do a baby, three dogs, and doting grandparents all have in common? Answer: two baby gates and a panicked mama. This describes our first Christmas with Indy.

Each first holiday with a new baby is special, and given the child-centric nature of Christmas, we were anticipating this holiday with the requisite level of excitement. Indy, always happy to be out and seeing new things, rode along snugly tucked against me in his baby sling as we cut down his first Christmas tree. I am guessing, however, that at six months the full adventure and spectacle of our annual ritual were probably lost on him. I tried to point out the draft horses pulling the kids in the holiday wagon, but I figured it was too much for him to take in. Like all parents, we wanted Indy's first big holiday to be perfect.

Once our tree was strung with lights and decorated, and the house was cleaned from top to bottom, we were prepared for my in-laws, who would soon be arriving for a couple of days to help us celebrate with Indy. As a very private person, Lawrence didn't reach out to his family too often and given that the dogs often overwhelm his parents, their visits are typically in the occasional category.

Pinball loved Lawrence's parents ever since the two weeks they stayed with him and Boo while we were picking up Indy. But he might have loved them a little too much. He can be a bit of a clingy dog when in love, and he frequently wouldn't leave them alone. He demonstrated his affection by trying to sit or stand on their laps, and at thirty-two pounds he really didn't qualify as a lap dog.

Porthos also loves Lawrence's parents, and at eighty-plus pounds, his love, too can be overwhelming. Although Porthos doesn't try to sit on laps, he leans a good chunk of his weight against the person delivering each and every scratch as he moans a low, gravelly moan of contentment, especially when he's getting an ear-noogie.

Boo loves Lawrence's parents, as well, but his limitations keep him from being too much competition for their affection, although he did manage to trip into the center of things every now and then.

Christmas morning arrived. Our biggest present that year was Indy rolling over at last and desperately trying to move himself by kicking his back legs. (At his baby shower I had referred to his legs as "back legs." Being so used to that distinction with dogs, I didn't even think about what I had said until everyone roared with laughter—so it stuck.) Indy was still trying to figure out that just kicking those legs was not enough—they needed to be underneath him, too. As a result, his only movement was a little scooting across the floor, fish-out-of-water style.

The wrapped presents were what would be expected for a

baby's first year: a gigantic box from Aunties Jill and Linda that seemed to take up a quarter of the living room, multiple boxes from the Gramampies (the collective name we gave Lawrence's parents since we are too lazy to say Grandma and Grandpa all the time), and several more items from us. Indy was like a child in a ball pit, but instead of balls, he was swimming in the growing pile of wrapping paper remnants and broken boxes. As everyone was reveling in the presents and the general spirit of the holidays, Indy's grandparents were on the floor with him, eagerly helping him wade through the mountain of gifts and their aftermath.

When people get on the floor around friendly dogs, they seem to take this as a directive to involve themselves in the proceedings. There on the floor in the overpacked living room were two adults, a baby, and three dogs all trying to occupy the same space.

Lawrence and I tried to stay out of it lest we add to the biomass clumping together too quickly to control. Pinball attempted to push his way between Indy and my in-laws, wanting his own attention from his favorite grandparents, while Porthos hungrily eyed the wrapping paper. Boo, not really sure where he was going but drawn to the noise and laughter, began bumping into the big back end of Porthos. I knew Porthos had only marginal tolerance for Boo's bumping into him and that tolerance dropped dramatically when the situation became complicated and stressful or a resource (like the wrapping paper) was involved.

Seeing the escalation of stressors and triggers, I could no longer do nothing and attempted to control the chaos. I directed Porthos away, sent Pinball out of the room with a *go sniff* command and then closed the gates, and guided Boo up onto his chair. I knew no one else saw what I was seeing, but Lawrence began to piece it all together when I started corralling the dogs and he saw *my* stress.

In the hopes of giving the dogs a little more space, I made the suggestion that it would be nice to take Indy outside to try his new sled from Aunties Jill and Linda. Lawrence pulled Indy back and forth around the barely snow-covered yard, while Boo walked along happily snuzzling Indy, whose eyes were almost completely covered by his new, slightly too big winter hat. Porthos and Pinball were left inside in separate rooms to calm down after all the excitement.

Through all the previous activity, I had seen Porthos turning quickly on Boo as Boo bumped into him. Then I watched Pinball goading Porthos with a hard stare and a whale eye over the wrapping paper that was quickly becoming a group resource. I knew Porthos couldn't take much more stress. With Type 1 diabetes, stress can either increase or decrease blood sugar, causing Porthos to have mood swings or seizures. Porthos's diabetic mood swings have often resulted in injury to another animal in the house. I knew to the outside observer the scene in the living room probably only looked like crazy doggie fun, but it was not, and without containment there would have been escalation.

After coming in from Indy's sled ride, Lawrence's father went out to sweep some snow from the deck. The dogs had all calmed down. Porthos and Pinball were back together and starting to become activated again, standing at the door watching my father-in-law. They tried to push each other out of the way under my mother-in-law's feet, who was also watching the snow removal. I could see the looks between the dogs intensifying like a scene out of *West Side Story*, complete with a kind of canine throwing of gang signs. I moved to physically split the dogs and I ended up inadvertently shooing my poor mother-in-law out of the way. I was sure she could only read my actions as being a crazy, overprotective dog owner—or just plain rude. I guessed rude since she and my father-in-law headed back to Pennsylvania an hour later. In the end, I would rather be seen as crazy, rude, or overprotective if it keeps me from being the owner of dogs who have made horrible mistakes.

In these situations, social propriety can get in the way of both parenting and pet training. We have to shut out the voices of doubt in our heads, and the comments from friends and relatives or even strangers on the street, in order to do what we know is best to keep our children and dogs safe. It doesn't always end with happy guests. We can try to make others understand our devotion to our dogs and their needs. However, if the person we are trying to explain things to is not of the same dog-mind as we are, it can be a tense uphill battle because they may not understand why we keep "those dogs." Or we could be faced with people who believe the simple act of once owning a dog imparts total canine wisdom and they know better how to interact and deal with our dogs. They could take it upon themselves to implement their training methods when in our homes or put pressure on us to follow their advice. I once had a client whose mother's friend decided to teach my client's dog who was boss and ended up in the mouth of that dog. Luckily, there was only a bruised arm and ego to go along with his comments that this dog should be gotten rid of. If he had followed my client's rules about her dog, no bite would have occurred.

I have difficulties making sure that even my husband follows our rules—and he is theoretically on board. It is much harder to have compliance with visiting friends and family members. A well-intentioned guest might say, "Oh, I don't mind a jumping dog." Maybe she doesn't mind dogs jumping on her with high-aroused excitement, but I mind. On the flip side are guests who try to use commands the dogs don't recognize and then wonder why the dogs don't comply. For example, when Pinball was standing on my in-laws, they looked him in the eye and told him *down* repeatedly. Both eye contact and repeated commands engage and encourage dogs in whatever they are doing, and may contradict the words people are using to stop an unwanted behavior. Obligingly, Pinball lay down on them because they told him through their words and gestures they were happy talking to him and to lie *down*. I reminded everyone the command was *off*, but it didn't stick. This inconsistency is frustrating for the dogs in the moment and over time can reduce their reliability on basic commands. Inconsistency is one of the biggest obstacles in dog training.

My in-laws, who are enamored of my son, are a good example of many family members who, when otherwise occupied with babies and little children on their visits, forget some of the dog rules. They may not remember the right commands and may not even see a dog altercation brewing beneath their feet. We cannot expect our guests to understand our rules or read our dogs the same way we do. It is our job to set the dogs up for success in these situations. To do that, we need to be the ones giving the commands instead of expecting the guests to know how. If our guests don't hear our instructions and do everything we asked them not to, or use all the incorrect commands, it is our job to take the dog out of the situation, either by bringing the dog over to us for a *settle* or putting him in another room or crate while the guests are visiting.

Sometimes, it is also our job to know when to put our fingers in our ears and hum a lively tune. A client of mine was afraid her little dog, who had a bite history, would not be safe around her grandchildren, so she called me. We began working on several training tools and exercises. One of them was to desensitize and counter-condition the dog to elicit a less fearful response when people arrived or departed. We worked with a Manners Minder (see details at the end of the chapter) to automatically reward the dog from anywhere in the house for relatively calm behavior. The dog was making nice progress, until my client's friend interjected that she was just rewarding bad behavior and the dog should be scolded and yelled at, as he does with his dogs. Feeling like she couldn't defend the process we were using, she listened to her friend and stopped the work we had been doing.

It isn't always easy for people to understand that when we are desensitizing and counter-conditioning we are not asking the dog for a lot of behaviors like *sits*, *downs*, or *stays* at first because in the beginning, the real work is not having the dog comply with basic commands. It is changing the dog's emotional response to a trigger from reactive to calm. And, when we are desensitizing and counter-conditioning we are not technically rewarding—we are using the positive association of the treats to change the negative association of the trigger. To the untrained eye it can be mistaken for rewarding the dog for nothing or for being "bad."

Unfortunately, after my client followed her friend's advice, her dog slipped back into highly reactive behavior, which resulted in the dog eventually biting her. Sadly, that dog did not survive her, or her owner's, mistake. This is a horrible and important example of what can happen when dogs get mixed messages in training. Please check with a professional with solid credentials before trying something a well-intentioned individual suggests. It could save your dog and your child from tremendous harm.

• • •

Training Tips You Can Try at Home

★ Arousal levels and stress
★ The arrival of guests
★ The *Go-say-hello* command
★ Front-clip harnesses
★ Choosing a professional dog trainer
   or behavior consultant
★ Manners Minder (also called the Treat & Train)

★ **Arousal levels and stress** go hand in hand, but often arousal can eclipse the typical warning signals that come when a dog is stressed (like those covered in Chapters Two and Five). There are things we would normally consider fun and exciting that are also stressful and can result in increased or decreased arousal levels in our dogs.

In our case on Christmas morning we had tight quarters, a lot of movement, and a louder-than-usual environment, resulting in all the dogs becoming over-aroused. Although the situation was fun and joyous, it stacked heightened arousal on top of the underlying stressors of illness for Porthos, chronic pain for Boo, and anxiety around resources for Pinball. The bigger body language expressions of heightened arousal were effectively louder than the subtler hard stare and whale eye that went on between Porthos and Boo, and Porthos and Pinball.

The challenge is to know what causes high levels of arousal in our dogs and how they react to it. Like humans, dogs can have heightened arousal as a result of sudden loud noises (good or bad), things that move quickly or suddenly, tight quarters, and overexcitement in the environment (good or bad). What is scary-loud to a dog may only be a bit louder than usual for us. Tight quarters for a dog would probably not be tight for a person unless he or she had claustrophobia. Overexcitement for some dogs could be four people having a typically boisterous family meal.

The calming and warning signals previously discussed are the canine way of saying, "Okay, that's scary, could you stop?" or "You scare me. Please back away."

The signals that tell us our dog is in a state of heightened arousal tell us our dog is so far over threshold he cannot communicate directly—much like a person crying or laughing. Both of these give the observer information but do not tell the observer something needs to be done, and often it is hard to understand crying or laughing individuals when they do try to talk through their emotions.

Indicators of high levels of arousal in your dog can include an increase in movement like jumping, pawing, circling, and pacing; a harder (chompy) mouth or increased saliva when taking treats; pinned-back or lowered ears; harder panting than usual; increased or decreased blink rates (not unlike people showing bug eyes, not blinking, or blinking a lot as if they have something in their eyes); or a lot of barking and whining. On the other end of the spectrum, some dogs may start to shut down, becoming quiet and disengaged when they would normally be interacting. All those indicators can obscure your dog's typical warning signals and lead you to conclude that your dog is just excited but fine, or quietly taking everything in when she may not be okay.

Owners have to watch and learn what their dog does when stressed and when over-aroused. If you are not sure of the meaning of the signals your dog is giving, fall back on my second rule, "When in doubt, get the dog out." If you were wrong and there were no issues, you can let the dog have access to the situation again. But if you were right, you will know because your dog will still be displaying signs of high arousal after coming out of the situation.

★ **The arrival of guests** often creates a great deal of stress for dogs. From a dog's perspective, the doorbell or a knock at the front door never occurs without something big following those sounds. Most of us don't mind our dogs barking an alert bark that tells us there is something happening at the door. However, most of us want the dog to stop quickly, and often the dog doesn't stop or the barking escalates.

Why? Because something always happens after the bell or the knock: someone comes in or goes out, a pizza arrives, Chinese food is delivered, or the kid's friends come for a visit. Your dog has been conditioned to the fact something always happens at the door and this spreads to any sound around the front door and all the guests who arrive there. If you can manage the rush of excitement and energized behaviors your dog demonstrates at and around the door, you can reduce your dog's stress, specifically her stress around guests.

☆ The simplest and most effective thing anyone can do when guests arrive is the thing they hate doing the most—have the dog in another room as the guests enter and then bring her out once she is calmer, provided your guests are okay with dogs. With multiple dogs and a narrow runway to our front door, I always choose to tell my dogs to go into other rooms. Sometimes Pinball and Porthos go to the master bedroom together, and sometimes Pinball and Boo go into the living room together. Once the guests are in and the dogs are calm, I let the dogs out to *go say hello* (see details below). Over time, they have calmed down faster and faster and as a result get to greet the guests sooner.

☆ When starting to bring your dog out to greet the guests, have her on a front-clip harness and leash (to help manage jumping) and then give her a *go say hello* command.

☆ Once she is calm with the guest, you can take the harness off. Once she knows the routine after repetition, she probably won't need the harness and leash at all for the initial greeting. The harness and leash can be left on if there is a need for ongoing management throughout the visit, but keep in mind that being on a tight leash distresses many dogs. If the dog is pulling to get to the guest, however, she is not ready for an on- or off-leash encounter.

☆ These practices allow us to keep our dogs' arousal/excitement levels lower at the beginning of a visit so they don't get overly cranked up with little chance of calming down easily.

☆ Once your dog has joined the guests, you can ask for a *settle* (this command, too, has to be practiced over time with family members before trying it out with strangers). If she *settles* around family, you have a prayer of getting your dog to relax in a roomful of strangers. Remember, your dog will not necessarily want to be with you and the guests for the whole visit. Have a puzzle toy (Kong, Twist 'n Treat, etc.) ready for your dog to enjoy on her own so you can send her into another room to quietly relax after a little visiting. Your dog might bark a bit, but if you have practiced this alone time when guests are not visiting and have given your dog a super-good puzzle toy, she will learn this separation is good and you can keep her stress levels modulated.

TRAINING TIPS

☆ When I recommend this technique to clients, they often reply, "But I want my dog to learn how to greet people." However, no dog can learn anything when they are so activated that they are unable to focus enough to process a *sit* command, let alone think of doing it. Allowing the guests to enter, give you their coats, food, and presents, and relax while the dogs are in another room teaches your dogs how to self-regulate. They can then be rewarded for their eventual and appropriate greeting. Every time your dog gets to jump on "Auntie XYZ," she is effectively practicing jumping for the next time. Your job is to not let your dogs practice these behaviors while setting them up for the most successful greeting.

★ The *go say hello* command is, for me, second only to *settle* in its ranking of importance in any home, but is most important in a home where many visitors will be coming over to see a new baby. This command teaches your dog exactly how to greet people. Your dog gets rewarded for being friendly around strangers and for greeting politely.

Initially teach *go say hello* with your dog on a front-clip harness and leash, as described above. If he starts jumping, simply walk him away and try again. The front-clip harness is essential because a back clip harness or collar allows for more pulling and creates a fulcrum/lever setup by which you are supporting your dog in midair.

☆ Start teaching this command with someone approaching you and your dog.

☆ Have several high-value treats closed in your fist.

☆ Place your hand on your dog's nose so he gets the full stink from the treats in your hand.

☆ When you feel him nuzzling your hand for the treats, say, "*Go say hello*," and gently pitch the treats in your hand from his nose to the feet of the approaching stranger (as if you are drawing a line between them in midair). Think of this as bowling, not baseball. Use an underhanded toss and try not to toss them through the person's feet, or your dog will end up halfway under the guest between their legs.

☆ Your dog will move forward with his head down and eat the treats while the person pets him. This teaches your dog to check in with everyone's feet and also conditions him to love strangers. (Who knows if the dog is wondering if every guest pees treats?)

☆ Once your dog is reliably moving forward without jumping, you can begin to do this command without the leash and harness.

☆ WARNING: Avoid doing this command with most dogs who are resource guarders. Because of Pinball's resource guarding, I couldn't take the chance that he would guard the treats and snap at the stranger trying to pet him. As a result, he never got to do too much of this and is still a work in progress regarding jumping.

☆ With some resource-guarding dogs, you can *lure* them sideways in front of the stranger and treat them directly from your hand as they stand with their side against the person's legs and get petted. Some resource guarders will be fine taking treats from you as they are being petted, and some will need to be rewarded after the petting so you don't elicit a resource-guarding response. Some resource-guarding dogs will not be able to have treats involved in this command at all.

☆ Not-so-friendly dogs? Many folks with dogs who are afraid of or aggressive with strangers choose to not have their dogs greet guests, except perhaps a few dog-approved friends. However, for the dogs who are on the tipping point of not-so-friendly and could go either way, the above exercise could be tweaked as follows to nudge the dog onto the friendly side:

» Instead of sending your dog to the stranger for petting with the *go say hello* command, let your dog see the stranger while he remains next to you and gets treats as you say, "*Go say hello*," as if you are telling him to *go say hello* from afar. Then have your dog *settle* near you while you visit with your guest. Keep this visit short and then let your dog go to a room or crate away from the stranger for his puzzle toy.

» After several repetitions of this command, your dog will be more at ease with the stranger, and you will be able to have him move toward the stranger for treats from you at first, but still not close enough for the guest to pet him.

» Finally, once your dog is happy to see the strangers, you can ask your guests to toss him some treats. Tossing is important because it is less scary (for most dogs) than having the stranger's hand coming right at them. Play this by ear and be ready to get the dog out by saying, "*Let's go*" and walking him away.

» Your dog will tell you with happy and relaxed body language when and if he is ready for the stranger to pet him.

» If your dog cannot do the *go say hello* command because of resource-guarding issues or because he is too fearful of strangers, it is time to consult a professional.

★ **Front-clip harnesses** are becoming more common and more easily available, compared to fifteen years ago when there was only one available online. There are a number of good brands to choose from. In a front-clip harness, the leash clips to the harness on the dog's chest in the front, which allows us to not engage the dog's opposition reflex when *loose-leash walking* or working on training skills like the *go say hello* command.

The opposition reflex, like any reflex, is not within conscious control. If we put pressure on our dog's neck or chest, he will reflexively push back against that. He cannot help it. This is why we have all seen dogs in the park or pet store on a choke collar looking as if they are strangling themselves, but they won't stop. They can't stop as long as there is pressure being put on their throat or upper chest. The front-clip harness does not put this pressure on the dog's neck or chest and so does not engage this reflex. If we use this harness when teaching *loose-leash walking*, we can easily stop walking when a dog is pulling without the dog dragging us; or we can use the harness to stop a dog who is jumping by putting a little pressure on the leash and walking away without worrying we will increase the dog's frustration by engaging that reflex.

In protection work, handlers typically want to engage the dog's opposition reflex because it makes their dog go after the "bad guy" faster and harder. We do not need this impulse in our pet dog, especially with our family or children. If using a front-clip harness becomes confusing or doesn't seem to be working, it is time to contact a training professional.

★ **Trainers, certified trainers, behaviorists, and consultants, oh my . . .** Choosing a professional dog trainer or behavior consultant is sometimes trickier than it sounds. The American Veterinary Society of Animal Behavior (AVSAB) has an informative position paper on this topic, and the American Society for the Prevention of

Cruelty to Animals (ASPCA) has an article on finding professional help that includes some helpful definitions of different professional terms.

☆ A certified professional dog trainer (CPDT) is certified through testing, fieldwork, and recertification every three years that requires continuing education. This certification is administered by the Certification Council for Professional Dog Trainers (CCPDT), which is not a teaching organization, but one that certifies only—thereby avoiding conflict of interest. This is patterned after the American Bar Association or the American Medical Association.

☆ Certified dog behavior consultants (CDBCs) are certified by the International Association of Animal Behavior Consultants (IAABC) after 500 hours of field work through a testing and peer review process. They are required to complete continuing education to recertify every three years. Like the CCPDT, the IAABC is an independent certifying organization. A certified behavior consultant canine (CBCC) is certified by the Certification Council for Professional Dog Trainers (CCPDT) after 300 hours of field work and testing; recertification is required every five years via continuing education.

☆ Applied animal behaviorists, certified applied animal behaviorists (CAABs), and associate certified applied animal behaviorists (ACAABs) have an MA, MS, or PhD in animal behavior. They have to meet additional requirements to be certified by the Board of Professional Certification of the Animal Behavior Society (ABS)—also solely a certifying organization.

☆ Veterinary behaviorists are veterinarians who have done further coursework and a residency program at a College

TRAINING TIPS

of Veterinary Medicine to become a specialist in veterinary behavior. It is important to remember that studying animal behavior is NOT required to earn a veterinary degree. Most veterinary training programs in the United States do not teach behavior. Keep in mind that a veterinary behaviorist is different from your regular veterinarian.

☆ Both the AVSAB and the ASPCA have some consistent suggestions for dog owners looking for a trainer or behavior professional.

» First on both lists is reward-based training—teaching by allowing dogs to earn rewards for doing the things we want them to. In other words, dog sits and you throw the tennis ball for him, or dog walks nicely on leash and you occasionally pop a treat in his mouth for keeping up the good work. To quote an AVSAB position paper, "Research shows that dogs do not need to be physically punished to learn how to behave, and there are significant risks associated with using punishment (such as inhibiting learning, increasing fear, and/or stimulating aggressive events). Therefore, trainers who routinely use choke collars, pinch collars, shock collars, and other methods of physical punishment as a primary training method should be avoided."

» A trainer or behaviorist should be able to explain things so they are easily understood.

» They should be involved in continuing education and able to demonstrate their credentials from nationally recognized credentialing organizations, including but not limited to, the ones listed above. Keep in mind the credentialing organization should not be the teaching organization. Just like a lawyer gets a law degree but has to pass the state bar separately, your trainer's or behaviorist's education and certification should come from different sources.

» There should be no guarantees. Asking for a dog training and/or behavior guarantee is like asking your children's teacher to guarantee that your son will be a successful lawyer or that your daughter will be a wealthy film producer when he or she grows up.

» Everyone's comfort is essential—yours and your dog's. I have been in the shoes of the novice handler when I took Boo to classes and remember trainers telling me to do things to my dogs that just didn't feel right. If you're not comfortable, keep looking for another trainer.

» You should be able to observe a class.

» Health is also important for everyone. Your trainer should remind everyone that a sick dog (or human) should not attend classes. I offer makeup classes for this reason and also because life sometimes gets in the way of training classes. Additionally, your trainer should check your dog's vaccinations. Vaccinations are a personal issue, but there are some that are mandated by the local township, and some that are important. Rabies is required by law, distemper and parvovirus are a must, and most dogs get the combination DHPP (distemper, hepatitis, parvovirus, and parainfluenza). There are other vaccinations you may want, but those above are the minimum.

» Your trainer should understand and help you understand that all dogs work at their own pace, and as long as you are making progress then you are on the right track. There is no way for a trainer to say that your dog will be able to do "XYZ" in two weeks or two months.

★ Manners Minder (also called the Treat & Train) is a machine that delivers treats automatically. It can be set to deliver a treat automatically on a schedule, or remotely with a button. This machine allows you to reward your dog when he is in another room, in his crate, or away from the door if you are working on good door manners. I like to use the Treat & Train with one dog at a time or only in single-dog households because there is a risk that multiple dogs could vie for the treats and there could be altercations as they try to get the treat from the machine. It is not an inexpensive machine and might not fit everyone's budget. In spite of that, it can be a marvelous device for teaching dogs to be happy in the crate, another room, or even the car.

CHAPTER NINE

The Visitors

....

By seven months Indy was progressing nicely and my only fret was financial. The recession had hit us hard, so day care was not feasible and the only socializing Indy had with other babies was the local Mommy & Me class, although it was mostly Lawrence who took him because my schedule generally had me out with clients during the afternoon. Luckily for Indy, Lawrence had no problem being the mommy and daddy at these times and quite enjoyed his time with Indy. Play dates, however, were not in the cards for us.

Our house was up a long, bumpy, and sometimes scary dirt road into the woods, which was not inviting for most people—even good friends are reluctant to visit. The weird hours I worked that changed from week to week, from ten in the morning to ten at night, weren't really conducive to making plans with folks. Lawrence's private nature meant he wasn't comfortable inviting anyone over or asking anyone at Mommy & Me to have him and Indy over. As a result, our visitors had been my friends and Lawrence's family, which made maintaining boundaries for the dogs much simpler than it would have been if we were having a number of little children visit frequently.

However, even with our limited guest list of cooperative adults who really wanted things to go well for Indy, I still had to guide the guests and the dogs so the high stress of visitors did not set us up for a regrettable moment, like the ones for which I frequently get calls from clients whose dog has "suddenly" bitten a relative, friend, or child.

The story usually starts with a party and the dog was just fine throughout the event, until the end of a long day when the dog bit one of the guests. We forget that while most of our dogs enjoy our guests, their tolerance for them is much shorter than ours. A long party with multiple people is just the ticket to push normally patient dogs to the breaking point, especially if the visitors are young children. Kids have a tendency to run around pushing the dogs' "chase-me" buttons. And their play screaming can often scare dogs and ignite their excitement levels. I have to remind clients that many interactions between a child and a dog are often rough or inappropriate from the dog's perspective, and just because a dog tolerates it today doesn't mean she will tolerate it tomorrow.

Indy seemed to have no issues with the fact that all of our visitors were adults. He reveled in it, happy to see everyone and turn on his charm—also known as the dimples. Once he smiled and engaged the power of the dimples, everyone was under his spell. He was happy and full of laughter at any silly face or any version of a rude noise one could make.

He was also starting to look forward to story time, which Lawrence claimed was more like performance art, when I would read books like *Click Clack Moo*, or *Love Monster*. Whether my animal noises were good didn't matter—they entertained Indy and that was enough. Story time was always followed by Indy happily falling asleep while staring at the stars manufactured by the plastic turtle at the foot of his bassinet.

Beyond Mommy & Me, the roles Lawrence and I played as his parents continued to be off-kilter from the usual Mommy and Daddy roles. Lawrence was still working from home most days and my schedule remained unpredictable. Indy got used to both of us doing everything throughout the day, depending on who was available, not on traditionally assigned roles of mommy or daddy. He also began to understand that although I would not be coming home at a regular time every day, when the dogs barked wildly, it meant that Mommy was home. Soon I was greeted by three barking, bouncing dogs and a "Come get me" cry from upstairs, or jumping in the living room bouncy seat that demanded, "Pick me up, pick me up."

Routine, consistency, and boundaries are cornerstones in good dog training as much as in infant care and development. Sometimes they are established by timing—everyday home by five o'clock—but sometimes the routine is established by consistent events, rules, and boundaries. Regardless of how we do it, it is much easier to build routine behaviors and implement rules and boundaries before something goes wrong. The process of establishing them is our job and our responsibility with our own child. If I tell Indy, "No, you cannot reach for the dog when the dog walks away from you," or "Do not pet the dog on the head; he doesn't like that," or "No, you cannot grab the dog's fur and pull," I have the ability to offer Indy a timeout from the dog or send the dog away as a consequence if Indy doesn't follow my instructions. I also have the ability to say to Indy that he can play freely in the living room or the bedroom if the gate is closed and Porthos and Pinball are out. But what do you do when you have other children visiting? They may have dogs at home who are completely different from your dogs. They may have different rules regarding their dogs and they may not be inclined to follow your instructions and boundaries. Or they may try but forget and fall back on the rules they know. Parents should have a predetermined dog management strategy in place for kids visiting their homes, a strategy that sets the dog and the kids up for success.

All interactions between dogs and visiting children have to be monitored by us in the same room. One day, on a visit to a children's hospital, one of the two visiting teams was falsely accused of being involved in a biting incident. We were waiting in the vestibule to start our visit and a boy involved in the previous visit walked by, pointed to the dog, and screamed, "That's the dog that bit me!" Not only had that particular team not accompanied us on the visit in question, but no bite had occurred in the first place! I can only speculate about why the little boy said this, but it was his perception, and perception plays a formidable role in how an incident is described. Your dog's life could hang in the balance, not to mention your homeowner's insurance. If your dog is alone with a visiting child and suddenly you hear a cry and then find a wound, what can you really know about what happened? Did the dog bite? Did the dog scratch? Did the dog knock the child onto something? What were the full circumstances of the situation? Were they roughhousing, was the dog feeling the need to protect himself, or did the dog just get fed up? We cannot know the answers to those questions without being there, which means we cannot devise a strategy to prevent future episodes because we do not know the details.

As a parent, you know in the back of your mind which kids you will allow your child to play with, which ones can play outside safely, which ones need to play inside so they can be supervised, which houses your child can visit because you trust the parents' oversight, and who you'd rather have come over to your house instead.

You will need to have a similar breakdown for your child's friends regarding your dog. One friend might follow your directions, while another actively looks to push the dog's buttons, and a third might exhibit fear of your dog and won't be able to follow instructions because of those fears. It will take a bit of talking to the kids (and their parents) and watching them interact with the dog to be able to adequately determine which visitors can hang around with your dog.

The dogs that live with your children's friends need to be considered, too. What do you know about the disposition of your child's playmate's dog and what kind of management do their parents have set up?

Sometimes it's the grandparents' dogs who are being visited. It is not uncommon for Grandma and Grandpa to babysit in their own home, where they may have a dog or two of their own. In these cases, it is necessary for them to take the same steps parents would to train their dog to be safe and secure around their visiting grandchildren.

Parents have to remember almost half of all the children under the age of eight who are killed by dogs each year are fatally injured by dogs belonging to friends or relatives they were visiting. Ultimately, any dog who will live with, or be visited frequently by, children needs to be trained to be safe around kids; and their owners need to have reliable management systems in place. Reliable management with kids when there is not adult supervision means the dog is behind a closed and childproof locked door. When there is adult supervision, management could mean an adult staying close to the dog, or the dog being kept behind baby gates. The dog could also be tethered to the adult, but not tied out in the yard or somewhere in the house where the child has the ability to access the dog. Too many injuries and deaths occur when dogs are tied up and left alone.

For many parents the need for child care is complicated by the discomfort they feel in approaching the individual caring for their child and saying that they are concerned about the dog living in the home. Children and dogs are two of the touchier subjects to broach with anyone. It is imperative, however, that a reasonable conversation regarding the safety of a child being cared for by a dog owner does happen—whether the caregiver is family, friend, paid, or unpaid. It might easier to say, "Oh that's a good dog. There is nothing to worry about." But it is impossible to go back and undo any harm that might occur.

It is also dangerous to think that there is future safety based on past behavior alone. Past behavior is only predictive of future behavior if the dogs in question are consistently well managed.

A tragic incident occurred in March 2013 in Wisconsin when an eighteen-month-old boy named Dax went to his babysitter for the twenty-first and last time. In this situation the parents had asked the babysitter to always keep Dax separate from her dogs and keep the dogs kenneled. For twenty visits she had and things had been fine, but for whatever reason that afternoon the babysitter was carrying Dax in her arms as she let the dogs out into their snow-covered yard.

It is never possible to know the complete underlying cause of a dog attack. We can make our best educated guesses, but we can't ask dogs what they were planning. In this case the dogs began their attack on their owner—the babysitter—and then moved to the child. The dogs had never attacked their owner previously. I will leave out the gruesome details because the general overview is telling enough. The dogs were trained to a reasonable level of reliability regarding *sits* and going into their crates. They had no history of attacking people, but there was a report they were aggressive toward dogs. Good management had always been in place when Dax was there, yet on this day the management was let go just enough to allow the little boy to be killed horribly.

Many people surrounding this incident have focused on the breed of these dogs—both sides of the Pit Bull argument have taken a stand on this case. However, there are many different breeds of dog who injure and kill, so my concern is more with the management of *all* dogs around children until we know if the dog and child are well matched for safety.

I tell my students and the volunteers I work with at shelters that they have to follow their gut regarding their comfort with a breed. If they are concerned about a particular breed, they should make the personal decision to interact with that breed or not without guilt. Fear translates into our voice, body posture, and overall interactions with a dog—so if you're afraid, don't go there. I tell clients with Pit Bulls, Rottweilers, Dobermans, Mastiffs, and Shepherds that they will be under more scrutiny because of breed bias, than the owner of a Teacup Poodle, and they will need better-trained dogs as a result. In the end, parents should be allowed to make the choice of what dog they want their child exposed to. They also should be able to tell their babysitter, grandparents, aunts, uncles, neighbors, or the parents of their child's best friend that they don't feel comfortable with certain dogs for their own personal reasons.

I have a fear of bridges. I am pretty sure that bridge designers would scoff at this, reminding me of how safe and well constructed they are. And that means nothing to me—I am still afraid. I am betting the engineers shrug a bit but hopefully don't take it personally. It is not meant personally and we cannot take it personally if someone is afraid of our dog.

The best conversations about this topic should begin with "I," not "Your dog." It should be about us and our comfort, and about owning the fact that we are taking protective measures across the board for our child. A sample statement to begin the conversation might be, "I am taking some advice on dogs and kids, and pretty much every authority out there recommends high levels of management when kids are around dogs. I would love for you to take care of my son as long as he is well managed away from the dogs. What management is already in place?"

Another example could be, "Mom, I love you. I love your dogs, and I love my daughter. Statistics tell me to set up some management strategies for when we visit you so no one, your dog or my daughter, makes a mistake that could be bad."

Just as you would teach your child with a nut allergy to ask about ingredients before eating a snack, you can teach your child to say, "My mommy doesn't want me playing around dogs if we are not with an adult, or if we are running all around."

My hope is that more comprehensive conversations will occur between parents before something happens because it will inspire dog owners to think about what they can do—more training and/or more management.

Two of my favorite clients have adult children who all have children of their own. My clients love dogs and have had dogs for the past sixty years, and the wife volunteers for puppy-raising duties with a local service dog organization. Yet when they brought home a rambunctious and mouthy ten-month-old rescued Shepherd mix, they were worried for their grandchildren, who visit often. After I met the dog, I was worried for them *and* their grandchildren.

He was strong with a hard mouth, and I was bruised more than a few times when working with him. They had great management in place for him—an exercise pen that contained him completely in a gated kitchen. He was slowly given more and more access to the house as his behavior improved and he settled into the home. At first when the kids were visiting he was in maximum containment—in the pen in the gated kitchen. Months after we started working, I said it was time to introduce him to the grandchildren without physical management, although the grandmother was always with the dog when he was interacting with the kids. By slowly integrating him into this family, he didn't make any mistakes with the kids and eventually was wonderful around them. In fact, he lights up for the kids as he does for no one else. (They tell me he does the same thing when he sees me, but I bought his love with treats, unlike the kids, whom he just loves.) They have made such wonderful progress with this dog that during the summer when their pool is open, the grandkids and the dog all enjoy swimming and playing fetch with the pool toys. Even so, when the kids are there for extended stays, the grandmother limits their time with the dog to give him a break and is always present whenever the grandkids and dog interact.

Another client of mine had a sweet, lively Brittany Spaniel who had bitten her son and one of her son's friends. The bites were minor, but they were still bites and that worried her. I recommended the usual strategies, but she said the dog loved to be with the kids and she couldn't be with them all the time to supervise.

So I told her, "Your dog does not have to be with the kids all the time. And probably she would do better if she had a break from them."

Her answer was, "But I can't crate her all the time and that's the only way to keep her from being with the kids."

I instructed my client to break the dog's time up as follows: The dog could spend time with the kids when the owner could be there to monitor the play and interactions, and then the rest of the dog's time out of the crate when the kids were around would be spent tethered to the owner. The dog would be nicely rewarded for hanging out while tethered as Mom did the dishes, laundry, and other chores like picking up toys, dusting, working on the computer, or whatever was on the agenda for the day. After about a month of tethering, the leash came off and the dog was happily conditioned to hang out with Mom instead of following the kids.

In an example on the opposite end of the spectrum, I had a client with four small kids and a friendly lab. The two-year-old girl loved this dog and just wouldn't leave him alone. He had growled at her several times and already bitten her once when the mother called me. When I met the dog, I could see that he had some joint problems that were causing him discomfort. Pain can easily contribute to a dog reacting to the constant pressure of a toddler with warnings and bites. It took a long time to convince the vet to do an X-ray, but ultimately the dog had joint surgery. I instructed the mother never to let the kids and dog be alone together. She did a good job with this management and continued it, especially after the dog's surgery. Unfortunately, in a busy home with four young kids and a dog, the mother occasionally lost track of the dog, who always wanted to be with the kids. One afternoon, Mom was in the kitchen and the kids were downstairs playing. The littlest girl was petting the dog, who was cornered between a wall and an end table. The dog bit the girl in the face just under the eye, resulting in several stitches. Tethering in this situation would have saved the little girl trauma and scars and would have kept this dog in the home he loved. He was returned to the organization that bred him and placed in a home with no children.

• • •

Training Tips You Can Try at Home

★ Other people's dogs
★ Homeowner's insurance
★ Tethering
★ The *touch* and *come* when tethering is not an option
★ Applications of the *settle* command
★ When you start having play dates
★ When talking to your caregiver who has dogs

★ **Other people's dogs** can be a thorny issue. When it's your friend's dog, you can have an adult discussion with them and maybe it will go smoothly. But when the dog belongs to the family of your child's playmate, this kind of conversation becomes fraught with various interpretations and emotional baggage. Sometimes you can have a candid conversation with the dog's owners to determine if you are comfortable with your child playing with the dog loose in the home. You might prefer the dog to be managed, or you could also simply not let your child play there. Assumptions about breed don't help too much, but there are some questions that you can ask your child if you cannot ask the parent.

☆ A general question such as "How does the dog play with you?" is a good starting point, but you will probably need to ask more detailed questions like these:

   » Does the dog put his mouth on your hands, feet, or arms when he plays with you?

   » Does the dog jump on you and grab your clothing with his teeth?

TRAINING TIPS

» Does the dog bark at you in a low, kind of scary way?

» Does he chase you and nip at your heels?

» Has the dog ever growled at you?

» Do you chase the dog around?

An answer of yes to any of these questions does not mean the dog is dangerous, but it can mean that things might easily get out of control, in which case there is a high likelihood of injury.

Having a discussion with the dog's owner after collecting these details requires delicacy. The talk cannot start with, "I think your dog is dangerous." Instead, feel free to blame me and tell them that a trainer has indicated that dogs who play in the above fashion can make mistakes that can injure kids they are playing with. Tell them it would be safer for everyone to have the dog managed away from the kids or interacting with the kids only with adult supervision.

★ **A dog with a bite history can alter insurance premiums** or result in canceled homeowner's insurance, and risk local municipal fines and imposed sanctions like muzzles, leash restrictions, or more. As a dog trainer, I have business insurance through a nice man who specializes in animal-related insurance policies. On this topic, he was unequivocal when he said, "One-third of all homeowner's claims in the United States every year are dog bite–related."

★ **Tethering** can be a useful management tool, but it also presents some dangers and needs to be used carefully. When you tether a dog to yourself, attach the leash on a front-clip harness and tie the leash around your waist or loop it through your belt. There are

TRAINING TIPS

also some quick-release leashes that are designed to go around your waist and be clipped and unclipped quickly.

☆ When tethering your dog this way, make sure he is within your reach, meaning the length of the leash should be adjusted so you can still reach your dog to deliver treats or easily give him hand signals for *sits*, *downs*, and other commands.

☆ It is dangerous to tether more than one dog at a time. I am extremely careful about having multiple dogs around when tethering only one dog, and usually only do tethering with multiple dogs when I am tethering a puppy and all adult dogs are puppy-friendly. I don't tether one adolescent or older dog when other adult dogs are roaming free—it can leave the tethered dog feeling vulnerable around the other dogs and increase the likelihood of an altercation.

☆ I also don't tether with kids nearby. The purpose of tethering in a home with kids is to keep the dog away from the kids. Tethering while kids have access to the dog is potentially dangerous because the dog can feel out of control and unable to get away from something that might scare her. As soon as it is time for a tethered dog to interact with the kids, she either comes off her leash, or I let the leash drag so she is free.

☆ The upside to tethering is that you know precisely where the dog is and there are no mistakes. It is effective for management and useful for teaching the dog a default stay-by-me behavior.

★ The *touch* and *come* commands can be used when tethering is not an option. But remember, you will always need to be watching to see if the dog has ventured into the kids' play and if yes,

TRAINING TIPS

call her with your **come** or **touch** command. It is not nearly as fool-proof as tethering, but for some folks, tethering just won't work. If you find you need to keep calling your dog because she would rather be playing with the kids who are out of your presence, it is import-ant to follow those commands with a **settle** so your dog decides it is more valuable to hang out with you. You will need to pay your dog an adequate treat salary for this **settle** to convince her to hang out with you instead of playing with the kids, who I guarantee are doing something much more fun.

Parents should start practicing **touch** and **come** with their dog when their baby is small and having swing time or belly time. You can start by being next to the baby and allowing a friendly, gen-tle dog some **settle** time around the baby. Then move a couple of feet from the baby, call the dog with **come** or **touch**, and be ready with some great rewards. Repeat this practice a few times when-ever your dog is having time with your baby and it will proof those commands so you can use them as your child grows and becomes more interesting to your dog, or has friends over who will multiply the excitement or fear for your dog.

★ Applications of the *settle* command remind me of how we use our smartphones—*settle* goes everywhere with us and applies to many situations as it keeps reappearing throughout the development of our children.

☆ In the early stages, *settle* is used next to the baby for things like belly time, feeding time, diaper time, or story time.

☆ *Settle* helps you help the dog to be comfortable with all the relatives who will be coming over to see the new baby. Your dog can be *settled* with you while you visit or *settled* in another room entirely (usually with a puzzle toy).

☆ *Settle* allows your dog to be comfortable and happy being on the other side of a baby gate when he cannot be with you and the baby, or your company, but still be in the mix by not having to be closed in a different room.

☆ *Settle* also comes in handy because it allows you to keep your dogs with you instead of following the kids throughout their play dates with friends.

★ **When your child starts having play dates,** it becomes apparent what behaviors your dog needs to have proofed. Reliable commands will decrease around new kids and their parents because we have introduced something new to the situation. For example, you may see your dog not *sitting* on command when there are guests, even though he would normally *sit* without guests there.

☆ When you have a play date at your house, have some treats for your dog (one dog at a time, if you have multiple dogs) in a training pouch or your pocket and ask for *sits*, *downs*, *settles*, *go sniffs*, and *go say hellos*. Your dog will look at you a bit funny at first, but after a while the light bulb will go on and he will think, "Oh, here, too? With people over, too? Okay, I'm getting paid; I can comply."

☆ After a few repetitions, over a couple of play dates, of these commands with rewards, you can begin to fade the rewards out. But keep them handy in case the situation gets a little chaotic and your dog loses his focus. If this happens, use the *go sniff* command to get him out, close the gate, and ask for a *settle* on the other side of the gate— crisis averted.

TRAINING TIPS

★ **When talking to your caregiver who has dogs**—whether it's grandparents, babysitters, aunts, or friends—there are some key points that should be part of this discussion.

☆ Ask them to have gates, crates, or a designated closed room set up so they can control their dog's access to your baby and your baby's access to the dog when they are not able to monitor the interactions.

If they are using the designated room, it should have a door that closes and that kids cannot open if they are toddling or older. This room is as much to keep the dog safe as it is to keep the kids safe, and allows him to have a break from the kids.

☆ Ask them to work on simple commands like *sit*, *leave it*, *stay*, *wait*, *come*, and/or *touch*.

☆ Let them know that you are no more questioning their dog's training than you would be questioning their driving skills when you ask them to use a child seat while driving with your baby.

CHAPTER TEN

He Throws Things to the Dogs

··

Sometime in the nine- to ten-month period, Indy learned how to stand by pulling himself up on the sides of the crib or play yard. For most parents, this is a time of great joy as they begin to think about their baby walking. I, however, had mixed emotions as I considered what the next step would be—literally.

What I didn't realize was that even before that step, I had to consider the "game" that had developed. Indy tried it with all the dogs, but only Pinball responded. I will never know if Indy began the game or if Pinball demonstrated it by picking up an accidentally dropped toy and Indy caught on to what Pinball wanted because it seemed fun to Indy, too. While clinging to the sides of his play yard, Indy would look at Pinball hovering just outside the pen in a typical herding dog pose, crouched like a sphinx, ready to pounce. The two of them locked eyes, trying to anticipate each other's move, as if they were acting out *The Good, the Bad, and the Ugly*. Indy, of course, was Clint Eastwood, and Pinball was Lee Van Cleef. I could almost hear the iconic music in the background—the unspoken question of who would go first hanging in the air. Then I would hear the toy drop to the floor or see it go flying, and before I could pick it up, quick, nimble Pinball was whisking it away to other rooms. Sometimes he would hang out with it in the kitchen, giving me a look that said, "You know better than to try to take this, right?"

Almost all of Indy's stuffed toys were missing body parts—ears, tails, legs, and other pieces. Even the most sentimental toys that Lawrence bought as a type of sympathetic magic while we were still in the waiting period of the adoption process—Dot-the-Hippo, Harvey-the-bear, and Kukalaka-the-monkey—lost their clothes, and poor Harvey was without ears with one arm hanging by a thread. Although Lawrence was upset by the damage done to these totems, Indy didn't seem to care that his toys were going to the dog. He just happily enjoyed the game and still snuggled with the naked, armless, and earless Harvey.

The real issues with the toy-tossing game were threefold.

1. Replacing eaten toys could get expensive.

2. Some of the toys were plastic and Pinball could be swallowing sharp chunks of them. His favorites were the oversized Lego-like blocks. This, too, could get expensive in terms of veterinarian bills if Pinball swallowed some sharp piece of plastic and needed surgery, or worse, if he didn't survive a perforated intestine. Pinball had already eaten a host of inedible items, including an entire squeaker that he pooped out whole (I actually heard it squeak as it came out) and a piece of foam from a pillow that sent us to the emergency room (it came out on its own the next day and promptly expanded to its original size—expanding poop is not a sight I ever expected to see). However, sharp plastic was a different issue. If ever we thought Pinball was going to swallow something, we moved to intercept it in the chewing stage as quickly as we could without spooking Pinball. Which leads to issue number three.

3. If we were in a rush to get one of those toys back and didn't think about what we were doing, there could be another bite on Pinball's record. In light of this, we performed toy triage. If it was not a dangerous or expensive toy, we took an, "Oh well," approach and casually bought it back when Pinball seemed to be tired of it.

We used the phrase, "Whatcha got?" as our way of telling Pinball we were taking a peek from a distance—no need to panic. It seemed to work and we were able to continue the buy-back program of toys for treats by slowly moving the behavior to a more ritualized series of steps. We would say, "Whatcha got?" and then check to see what it was. If it was nothing dangerous, we walked away. If it was something dangerous, we said, "*Drop it,*" and Pinball would head for the green dog pillow in the dining room. His *drop it* ritual was still in place and he circled once or sometimes several times around, depending on how valuable the item was to him. Because of the volume of toys tossed to him, Pinball had regressed a little and I could no longer ask for the series of behaviors ending with the trick. Instead, I had to return to dropping a couple of treats and then reading his body language to be sure he was not going to try to grab the toy (or me) when I went to take it.

The only time things got gummed up was if Porthos was on the green pillow in the dining room. Then Pinball just didn't know where to go because he wouldn't share the pillow with Porthos. It was too much social pressure for Pinball. But Porthos's good skills and maturity worked in our favor, and all I had to do was tell Porthos to get off the pillow. He would comply and Pinball could complete his ritual.

Happily, neither Porthos nor Boo cared about the toys flung in their direction. So at least we only had to negotiate with one dog to retrieve the toys Indy was tossing for fun and as early lessons in gravity and commerce.

This Pinball toy buy-back program was happening multiple times every day and both Lawrence and I were tired of it. But Indy was having a blast and clearly so was Pinball, illustrated by the fact that he was putting on enough weight from the treats that I had to cut back on the food in his bowl each meal.

When the game began, Pinball looked forward to the toy toss, and Indy learned he could toss from inside his play yard, or over the gate when he was roaming free in the living room. He even started to aim for Pinball. But as Indy got stronger, the toys flying in Pinball's direction began to get bigger and scarier, usually hitting the wood or tile floor with a loud crash (that sometimes startled even us bigger humans, too). I began to see fear creeping into Pinball's demeanor even when smaller toys flew. The fear of the larger, more frightening toys was starting to overshadow the joy of the smaller playthings. Soon nothing about this game would be fun for Pinball and Indy would become a source of fear for him.

Fear is one of the main reasons dogs bite. I could not let Pinball, who had demonstrated he would bite, become afraid of Indy. Fear was just not an option—it had to be controlled. However, telling a ten-month-old little boy not to throw his toys over the play yard or the gates would be futile until he eventually learned a better game, but that would take too long for Pinball. I couldn't take away all Indy's toys to make Pinball feel safe. The only management option left was to completely exile Pinball from any Indy-time, which would defeat all my efforts to ensure they became best buddies.

It was time to consider medication for Pinball. In the strictest approach to desensitization and counter-conditioning it is imperative we keep the subject (Pinball) subthreshold. That is the point at which any of us can tolerate something that scares us. In contrast, over threshold is the point at which we cannot even think straight because we are so scared, worried, or distracted. In the configuration of our home I could not keep Pinball subthreshold without undoing the bonding that was going on between him and Indy.

Medication for Pinball had been on my mind from the moment Lawrence told me about the October bite that had me redoubling my behavior modification efforts. Pinball's fears were increasing in variety: some strangers in the home, the bigger toys flying at him, Indy crying, and any odd noises Porthos made that might mean he was ill. Pinball even generalized this one to the point at which he would react when I hiccupped—because it sounded like one of the first sounds Porthos made when he was ill. With his list of fears growing so long and having so many components, Pinball was fearful almost constantly and subthreshold was becoming an ever-shrinking sliver of his life.

In short, we have to look at the dog's fears and his environment and then ask if behavioral modification alone will be unable to do its job because we can't keep the dog subthreshold. It was time to consider antidepressants for Pinball, even with the risks they posed.

Traditional antidepressants work for dogs in a similar manner as they do for people, and just as in humans there can be unwanted and sometimes negative consequences. We have all watched commercials for antidepressants on television and scratched our heads when the side effects are listed—increased depression, thoughts of suicide, and other paradoxical effects. In dogs, paradoxical effects can include increased anxiety and increased aggressive behavior (also called de-inhibition), as well as the standard side effects of increased risk of seizure and loss of appetite among others.

It is not uncommon for my clients to say to me, "This behavior modification is a lot of work. Isn't there a pill I can give my dog?" There are loads of pills, but the advice of a veterinarian is essential to be sure that the side effects of these medications are clear. Sometimes the medication is worse or more complicated than the original issue, and sometimes one medication just won't work while another one might. Regardless of medication, behavior modification will still have to be implemented. I have had plenty of discussions with local veterinarians and behaviorists about the dogs whom antidepressants didn't seem to help, usually because of a lack of behavior modification in conjunction with the medication.

Prescription drugs alone are rarely the only answer. That would be the equivalent of someone having a gastric bypass surgery but not altering his or her eating habits according to the behavioral protocol.

In Pinball's case I already had a behavioral modification protocol in place and knew where I had to begin additional protocols for the scary flying toys. I was confident the exercises could work because they were working on certain levels, but our success was decreasing due to the difficulty of keeping Pinball from going over threshold. He was always revved up and we needed him in neutral. If I could not get him subthreshold, the current behavior protocol would start to go in the opposite—negative—direction. Just as we can turn scary triggers into happy times through counter-conditioning, happy times can turn into scary triggers. It was quite possible that all the happy associations with Indy I had built for Pinball would be turned into scary associations if I couldn't get Pinball to a more level, subthreshold state of mind.

I had the unfortunate opportunity to experience this fine line between good and scary firsthand with a shelter dog named Wesley. He was a smart, engaging dog who enjoyed certain people in certain situations but who was also a fierce resource guarder, under socialized, and at times difficult to touch safely.

Because he needed medical attention for a dewclaw issue, I worked to get him muzzle happy, meaning he would happily and easily put his nose into the muzzle and wear it without fussing. When he was happy with his muzzle, we took him to the vet. I knew I would need some super-high-value primary reinforcers, the kind I would use for desensitizing and counter-conditioning, to keep him distracted during this procedure, so I brought yogurt for him. He could lick it while wearing the muzzle and he loved it until the vet got vexed with his squirming and hit him. At that point Wesley stopped taking the yogurt and turned to snap at the vet. I, of course, never took him to that vet again, but Wesley refused to eat yogurt for the rest of his life. Fear is a powerful lifesaving emotion and its ability to spread like a disease cannot be underestimated.

Trying to decide if medication was right for Pinball left me with a great many intellectual waves of doubt because I had experience with clients whose dogs did not do well on medication prescribed by a veterinary behaviorist and lost their lives due to behavioral and medical complications. Pinball was at risk either way—giving him antidepressant medication could increase his aggression or cause seizures, to name two contraindications, but not giving him the medication would leave him increasingly afraid of Indy without any relief.

My hope was that medication, in addition to helping decrease Pinball's anxiety in the face of the flying toys and some strangers, might also resolve some of his resource guarding. I had been mulling over Pinball's guarding, along with those of a couple of other resource guarders with long bite histories, and in each case their guarding was made worse by an increase in their stress levels. One became more stressed when family dogs came to visit for the weekend, and another (Wesley) was made worse over time in the shelter—arguably a stressful place for most dogs. It was at this point that all the pieces from all my resources-guarding cases fit together and I knew that there was an anxiety component to resource guarding, much like the anxiety felt by a person with a hoarding disorder. This decision regarding Pinball's future left me feeling that I was stranded in the desert, knowing I had to go in some direction or die of thirst, but each direction held peril. I went with my typical damn-the-torpedoes approach and we started Pinball on Prozac.

Lawrence and I discussed it at length. I explained what we would need to look for in terms of changes in Pinball, from de-inhibition to seizures, and we were both on watch for any negative change in behavior.

My concern is that parents reading this chapter will think, "Okay, new baby. Dog needs medication." That is not at all the case. It is important to remember that when we read about the worst cases of dogs biting and attacking children, there are often statements from friends and family members describing a dog who loved the child. Some dogs will adjust to their new human babies better than others. There is a big range in adjustment levels and then there is the danger zone, where Pinball was. Pinball was a biting dog with some intense fears that he couldn't escape because they surrounded him daily. If parents find themselves in a similar situation, they need to consult a veterinary behaviorist.

The introduction of Prozac was a welcome relief for Pinball and all of us. Despite the daily onslaught of hurtled toys, he responded better to desensitizing and counter-conditioning. He was more at ease around the bigger soaring toys and learned he could easily move away from the landing areas. Happily, his resource guarding was much more manageable as well. He began to release stolen toys more quickly and he had a generally more relaxed attitude about the relinquishment of his ill-gotten goods.

Training Tips You Can Try at Home:

★ Eating sharp items can be dangerous for dogs
★ *Leave it* and *drop it*
★ "Whatcha got?"
★ Over threshold and subthreshold
★ Medication for a behavior issue

★ **Eating sharp items can be dangerous for dogs** because either way a sharp object passes through your dog's system can be an issue. If vomiting is induced, the object could tear up the esophagus, and, if the item passes though the entire digestive system, it could tear through the intestines. Ultimately, if you think your dog will ingest sharp objects, a program of management of these objects and the dog that emphasizes super-reliable ***drop it*** and ***leave it*** commands (along with having your veterinarian on speed dial) is in order. Your veterinarian can tell you when to panic and when to wait and see. But in the end, prevention is the best option to save your dog's life.

★ **I spoke a bit about *leave it* and *drop it*** in Chapter Four, but now it is time for detail.

☆ *Leave it* means your dog will look away, walk away, or just ignore anything you tell her to disregard.

» Start with a treat either closed in one hand or under your hand on the floor. Tell the dog to ***leave it***. Be patient and don't repeat the command. It may be a while, long enough that you will doubt she will ever look away, but she will. Once your dog has looked away, praise and reward her immediately from the hand that's not concealing the treat. Repeat this exercise a few times.

» Then start putting the treat under your foot and tell her to *leave it* and repeat the waiting game until she looks away. Then praise and reward.

» The next step is called the spider. Put the treat under your hand with your fingers acting like the legs of a spider encapsulating the treat, like you're making a clawing gesture on the floor, as you say "*Leave it*." Your dog will be able to see and smell the treat. She will push your fingers around to get it. Hold the line and don't let her get it. When she gives up, praise and reward her with a treat from the other hand.

» Once you have worked through the spider and your dog is happily leaving everything put there, it will be time to do the tossed treat *leave it*. Have your dog on leash for this exercise. Toss a treat just out of her reach while you tell her *leave it*. Flying food is harder to resist than food politely placed on the floor (flying anything is harder to resist for most dogs). She will try to get it, but you will just hold onto that leash and not let her move toward the treat (a front-clip harness is essential for this). Once she realizes she cannot get it, she will turn back to you as if to say, "Hey," and at that point immediately praise and reward this behavior.

» On the road, or throughout the day, you will need to have treats available so that when you say *leave it,* your dog can have an instant reward for complying, and you can have a quick attraction if you need it to *lure* the dog away from whatever she should leave.

» This command will take some time because your dog is programmed by nature to want to get things first and ask questions later. Dogs are as much scavengers as they are the majestic hunters we imagine. Persist and it will pay off. Even Pinball has learned *leave it*.

☆ *Drop it* is actually a little easier than *leave it* (for most dogs). I suspect it has to do with the fact that the emotion of wanting something creates a higher motivator than the emotion of having something.

» Begin your *drop it* games by strolling around a room or your backyard with your dog and for no good reason (when he is not following you around) suddenly say "*Drop it*." At the same time, fling a bunch of super-high-value treats on the floor. Encourage the dog to come over to the treats and eat them with you helping him to find the treats with your hands. This conditions the dog to love hearing the phrase *drop it* and having your hands right in front of him because your hands are helping, not taking away anything. Remember, he has no object in his mouth at this time; he is just hanging out with you, sniffing, scratching, or daydreaming.

» After doing this exercise several times, you can begin to work with objects. I like to start with something easy like a small wad of paper towels or Kleenex because if the dog swallows either of these, it will easily come right up or out—no harm done. Drop the paper towel onto the floor and once your dog has picked it up, take several stinky treats in your hand, say, "*Drop it*," and place your hand in front of your dog's nose (provided he has no bite record and no resource-guarding tendencies. If he does, work only with the *drop it* games above.). Wait, but not as long as for *leave it*. Once your dog spits out the paper towel, drop the treats on the floor to the side of the dog so that he turns his head to get the treats and you can retrieve the paper towel.

» Meanwhile you will continue to randomly say *drop it* for no good reason, when no object is involved, and with super-high-value rewards, to keep the dog happy with the phrase and what he probably considers a great game.

» Once the paper towel *drop its* are going well, you can start adding in other objects like flip-flops (which are just dog toys that we happen to wear), socks, underwear, towels, wash clothes, and so on. Surprise the dog by seeming to mistakenly leave these items around or let them fall. When your dog picks them up, be ready to ask for the *drop it* and have the stinky treats—now you can either hand your dog the fistful of treats for the *drop it* or the toss the treats on the floor. If your dog does not pick these items up, praise and reward her anyway (remember, if you like what she is doing even if you have not asked for it, praise it and reward it).

» When your dog seems to be stealing things to parade past you as if to say, "Hey, see what I got, human—maybe you should say those magic words?" it is time to start chaining behaviors. For example, *drop it*, then *down,* then *wait* or *settle*, and then the reward. Your dog, like many humans, will naturally want to perform the least amount of work for the most payoff. As a result, you will begin to get more *settles* and less stealing of objects, provided you are paying attention and praising and rewarding the *settles* when they happen.

★ **"Whatcha got?"** is really a conditioned cue that means you are checking in to see what the dog has. Sometimes you will let him keep whatever he has and sometimes you will ask him to *drop it*. The benefit of having this interim conditioned cue is that it allows you to let your dog know you are checking in to see what he has without spooking him into running under the bed, or posturing with a growl, snarl, or snap. Once a dog understands that "Whatcha got?" doesn't mean he is losing his toy—or if he does he will be getting paid for it—it allows you to tone down any possible escalation of guarding or aggression by the simple act of looking directly at what the dog has.

> ☆ Simply say a phrase like "Whatcha got?" or another easy-going query phrase when your dog picks anything up. Say it in a happy tone that does not introduce tension into the situation. Then, after you have looked at the item without reaching or bending, you may walk away and have no further interaction with your dog over the item, or you may execute a *drop it* for rewards.

★ **Over threshold and subthreshold** are states of being that dramatically alter behavior. An example of subthreshold in humans would be a person driving along a road he knows well during the daytime in good weather. His senses are alert because he is engaged in an activity, but he is calm and able to talk to passengers or listen to the radio without it affecting his driving. However, if we add nighttime, bad weather, and two deer running out in front of the car, we now have a driver who is over threshold. He probably didn't even hear the passenger scream when the deer appeared; he couldn't tell you what song was on the radio at that moment; and for a good length of time after this incident his heart was racing, his stomach was upset, and he was jumping at the slightest movement along the side of the road. If you gave him directions at this moment, it is likely he couldn't remember a simple sequence.

When our dogs have triggers that stack, as in the second human example above, they, too, become over threshold and cannot think straight. For example, when we have people over on the Fourth of July with firecrackers in the backyard and small children running around with sparklers, we need to understand that many dogs will likely be over threshold. They will not be able to make the best decisions in that moment. It is important to take stock of each of your dog's triggers and have a good idea when they are starting to stack up so you can give your dog a break from the situation.

★ **Medication for a behavioral issue** is a personal decision that has to be discussed with your veterinarian. The problem that folks run into is the wide variety of opinions on the subject. We know from clinical evidence that many dogs benefit from behavioral medication in conjunction with behavioral modification. However, the advice from veterinarians can range from "I don't believe in giving dogs behavioral medication" to "Better living through chemistry."

☆ You will want to discuss any issues your dog is having with your veterinarian. Be prepared with information on the subject and get a second opinion, especially that of a veterinary behaviorist, if you have unanswered questions.

☆ There is a lot of information online to help you research the subject. I recommend starting with the ASPCA website and their article "Behavioral Medications for Dogs." It is probably the most comprehensive overview of behavioral medications for dogs, describing both the maladies and the treatments. Common treatment medications include benzodiazepines, monoamine oxidase inhibitors (MAOIs), tricyclic antidepressants (TCAs), selective serotonin reuptake inhibitors (SSRIs), and serotonin (5-HT) agonists.

☆ It cannot be stressed enough that these are not magic pills. They will need to be given with the oversight of a veterinarian and a trainer or behaviorist with experience enough to help with the behavioral modification protocols.

TRAINING TIPS

☆ A word of caution here: Many veterinarians still prescribe Acepromazine for phobias. It is not an anxiolytic drug; it is an antipsychotic that is used as a chemical restraint for dogs. It can actually increase your dog's fears in a variety of situations. In her September 2004 article for *DVM360* magazine, Dr. Karen Overall specifically outlines the dangers of this drug for dogs with phobias.

"I know that the common "treatment" for storm and noise phobias and veterinary office visits is Acepromazine. In truth, I wish this medication would be placed at the far back of a top shelf and used only exceptionally. Acepromazine is a dissociative anesthetic meaning that it scrambles perceptions. Ask yourself if a scrambling of perceptions will make an anxious or uncertain dog worse or better. It's always worse, and we make many if not most dogs more sensitive to storms by using this drug. In part this is also because sensitivity to noise is heightened.

This is a recipe for disaster for these dogs, and, in fact, they learn to be more fearful and more reactive because of these associations. . . . it makes most of my really fearful and really reactive patients worse, so all sorts of other drug combos can work better and do less harm than is done by the routine use of Acepromazine."

CHAPTER ELEVEN

First Birthday Party and Measuring Sticks

....

In Indy's first year everything seemed to go so quickly, yet it felt as if we had been a family forever. Happy and easygoing in his first year, Indy had shown us he was inquisitive and interested in his surroundings, whether it was the zoo, aquarium, or wholesale club. He loved flirting with anyone we met along the way. Of course, his dimples didn't hurt. They seemed to have magical powers to make everyone fall in love with him.

He happily showed us, through culinary exploration, that he was an eating machine who enjoyed jerk chicken, Chinese food, guacamole, chili dogs, and more. On Lawrence's first Father's Day—just a week before Indy's first birthday—I took Lawrence out for one of his favorites, Indian food. Unsure if Indy would eat much, we were prepared to give it a try and see how it went. Still a food trouper, Indy devoured his kheema naan, which is bread stuffed with spicy ground lamb. I shared my chicken tikka and saag paneer with him, but we held off giving him Lawrence's lamb vindaloo (the hottest of the spiciest).

As we arrived, a large Indian family was also walking into the restaurant with a little girl about Indy's age. Clearly, they were celebrating Father's Day, too, and we casually remarked on that to each other as we went to nearby tables. When Indy needed a break from sitting for so long, I got him up and walked him around a bit. He wanted to flirt with the little girl, but she was busy eating her chicken nuggets and french fries. We had a laugh about that and patted ourselves on the back until we remembered the words of our pediatrician about the eighteen-month finicky phase. We knew that his gastronomic openness was only a temporary phase, but we will take any and all culinary victories.

Indy had been assessed by the New York State Early Intervention Program and determined to be developing normally, but he was still at risk for developmental delays due to some prenatal issues. The process in these cases was to have a New York State Child Find Nurse come to the house every three months to assess his development so we could address any delays as soon as they occurred. His nurse was happy with his progress and all in all we had a lot to be grateful for by the end of his first year.

Planning Indy's first birthday party was a little emotionally overwhelming. We were not sure we would ever be able to share a first birthday with a child of our own. For many families, the first birthday is a huge event for which the planning often starts before the baby is even born. These parties often include the arrival of many adults, kids, and new items in the form of presents. There is a lot of activity, commotion, and chaos, as with any major social occasion.

Functions like these can cause a level of anxiety in dogs that makes them more likely to act in an inappropriate or dangerous way. The tragedy in Las Vegas between Onion and Jeremiah on Jeremiah's first birthday should forever be a cautionary tale about the potential heartbreaking fallout of the stressors that go along with the first birthday party, or any party, when dogs are around small children for extended periods of time.

My internal emotional soup combined the excitement of Indy's first birthday, the stress of a party in general (I'm not much of a party person), and the incident involving Onion and Jeremiah floating like a specter in the back of my mind, making it difficult for me to plan his party.

As is my approach to big-ticket-stress items, I worried and fretted about where to have it, who to invite, and how to keep the dogs safe and happy while keeping the guests safe as well. I knew I would have to sequester Pinball for the safety of the guests, Porthos for his own safety, and maybe even Boo for his own safety, too. Boo would want to interact with the guests but would be bumping into everyone and everything as the house got more and more crowded. In the end, I got lucky and skirted the dreaded dogs and birthday party conundrum when my friend Teddi offered her home for Indy's party.

She has the perfect house for entertaining and only one easygoing dog. Jill and Linda offered to help out, so Indy's favorite aunties—Teddi, Jill, and Linda—took on the bulk of putting together his first birthday party. It was a small occasion with only close friends and Lawrence's parents. Indy's favorite New York City aunties, Michele and Laura-Ann, came up from the city and brought marvelous cakes from Good Enough to Eat (where Michele is the chef) for Indy to wear—although he did manage to eat a good portion, too. Lawrence was happy with our choice of meal, his second favorite food in the world—ribs. Which Indy ate with gusto.

Milestones allow, or force, us to look back and assess the time between them, and Indy's first birthday had me reviewing the year on many levels.

How had we done in terms of his development, eating, and health? Pretty well.

Was he happy? Yes.

Did he feel loved? I hoped so.

How did Indy feel about the dogs and the cat? He loved them!

How had the dogs done in terms of settling in with him? Those results were mixed.

Boo was his usual kid-loving, go-with-the-flow self and he loved Indy. I was able to start teaching Indy how to gently pet Boo, who was as usual a trouper in all situations. He tolerated and even enjoyed Indy's clumsy petting.

Porthos loved Indy, and although his size was still an issue, he was always tender with him. When Indy and I would sit with Porthos on our king-sized bed, Porthos would stretch out to nuzzle and sniff Indy eagerly but gently. Even so, given Porthos's stress-related health issues, these encounters were kept short and sweet to prevent triggering a diabetic or OCD event.

Pinball followed his little boy all around the house and, after medication, was less on guard when he saw large baby toys flying in his direction. He was learning to compensate by using his quick and agile skills to maneuver around and away from the toys thrown at his head, or baby hands grasping over the play yard and gates.

I had to conclude that at the end of the first year, we had not done too badly. We were at the point where the dogs could move unrestricted throughout the house, even in the living room or master bedroom, when Indy was happily playing in his play yard. Parked next to the play yard like a sentinel, Porthos would often sit happily panting in Indy's direction. Pinball would never miss an opportunity to lick Indy's feet and hands when they were within range, as he passed the time between stealing toys. All in all I was happy with the dogs' acceptance and love of Indy. But I knew there would be more hurdles as soon as Indy started walking on his own.

For me the year had been a juggling act that I had expected but not truly anticipated. I had known things would have to be shifted and time would be crunched, but I didn't understand the emotional and physical toll all that would take. I felt like one of our ceiling fans during a hot summer, always in constant motion and showing the signs of wear and tear as a result.

Things that I had always been quite good at BB (Before Baby) were left by the wayside. Business filing that used to be immaculate was a mess beyond belief. Our laundry room looked more like a communal closet. Getting the laundry done didn't always leave time to put the clean clothes away; we were just glad they were clean. And house cleaning was more like just picking up the bigger clumps of dog hair between pre-holiday vacuumings. Dusting meant strategically blowing over the dustier areas as if they were pesky birthday candles that wouldn't go out.

But probably the biggest personal challenge during this first year was my back. Indy had started to disassemble his Pack 'n Play (which we used as his crib) little by little. One morning when he was about ten months old, we went in to wake him up and he had taken everything out of the Pack 'n Play and was sleeping in the hammock formed by the folding mechanisms at the bottom. (For anyone unfamiliar with a Pack 'n Play, it was as if he was sleeping in the folding ribs of an upside-down umbrella.) Why it had not folded on him is a mystery and a minor miracle. That was the end of that.

We bought a kid's mattress and another play yard and made him a sleeping pen with a snuggly rug, mattress, blankets all over, and toys within reach. He preferred to sleep on the floor, and I suspected he couldn't figure out why the big mattress was hogging up all the good floor space. This arrangement, odd as it might be, worked out perfectly for him. But for me, lifting that big boy straight up from the floor several times a day was beating the crap out of my back.

Several of my disks had been bulging for years, and the ongoing process of picking up Indy sent the L4 and L5 disks into a state that my pain management doctor simply referred to as "quite impressive." Just a month before Indy's first birthday, I couldn't walk, let alone pick him up, for two weeks straight and then I only had limited movement. Once I was up and walking again, I had to jam aqua therapy sessions between teaching classes, seeing private clients, taking care of Indy, doing household chores, and going to doctor's appointments—never mind planning the party. Indy is very lucky his aunties stepped in to take care of that because I still don't recall exactly how we got food on a regular basis during that month.

Time for training the dogs was squeezed out of the priority positions—it had to be crammed somewhere in between everything else, and there was not any in between left. Instead, training had to become a part of everything. I had treats everywhere—in the nursery, in the master bedroom or bathroom (they migrated), in the kitchen and dining room, in my office, in the living room, next to the back door, and probably other places I have forgotten. In short, I was *luring* and shaping everywhere and could ask Pinball to do anything anywhere and be able to pay him for doing it without missing a beat. If I was cooking something for Indy and he threw a toy over the gate, Pinball would pick it up. If it was one of the dangerous ones—no problem. I would calmly ask Pinball to *drop it*, take a treat from the kitchen island container, walk to the pillow, deposit the treat, pick up toy, and return to cooking—not even ten seconds in total time. If I was reading a book to Indy and Pinball came into the nursery and lay down next to me, I shaped that by handing him a treat for an unrequested *settle*. I had become the parent I counseled so many times who said, "I just don't have time to do the training." And, as I predicted, it wasn't perfect or pretty—but inserting training into every activity worked!

There are, however, some parents who seem to pull everything together and never break a sweat while they manage to dust, organize, and not tear a disk in their lower back. I witnessed this perfect family early one morning when Boo and I were in Los Angeles for an interview on Marie Osmond's show. As Boo and I stepped out of the hotel to give him a quiet potty before the long flight back to New York, a woman jogging with two Border Collies, one on either side, whizzed past us, followed closely by a man pushing a baby in a BOB running stroller. They were clearly all together and seemed quite happy and content.

If each of us could incorporate our own passions into activities with our dogs and our children in such a way as these parents seemed to have, we would all be perfect. But alas, most of us strive to do a little here and there so we can build a routine that takes care of at least some of the chaos. Lawrence is always reminding me to not let the perfect be the enemy of the good. So if it works but it isn't perfect, it's fine as long as it is on the way to the final goal, hopefully closer to perfect.

Ironically, the day before Boo and I left for our big Hollywood television appearance, the economic downturn and outsourcing took another IT banking job from Lawrence. I had come to accept that we were definitely a good-news–bad-news family—there is never one without the other. We were now a one-income home, trying to figure out the economics of how we could make that work.

The issues that usually plagued working or wannabe working mothers are now cross-gender concerns in many homes. Deciding whether it is more cost-effective to work and pay for child care or to stay home no longer applies only to women. As with so many things, there were two sides to this new coin. On one side, Indy had his father home with him all day without the distraction of trying to work while caring for a baby. I was also still working from home, so he frequently had us both. On the other side of the coin, no matter how much you love your spouse, child, and pets, everyone needs a break at some point. I could swear that sometimes I would look at the dogs and be sure they were saying, "Don't these humans need to go out somewhere?" In short we had added another couple of stressors to our lives and the dog's lives, and all I could do was hope there wouldn't be fallout.

• • •

Training Tips You Can Try at Home

★ How long do I have to treat my dog?

★ Which is faster, *luring* or shaping?

★ How do you exercise baby, dog, and yourself?

★ *Loose-leash walking*

★ Fetch

★ When will you be able to let your dog and baby play together?

★ **When I advise parents to have treats** all over the house for integrated dog training, it usually leads to a common question, regardless of dog-baby issues—how long do I have to treat my dog? This answer depends on three factors. First, how good are you at remembering to use the same cue every time you want a specific behavior? Second, how good are you at consistently rewarding your dog after verbally praising your dog? Third, how difficult is the behavior for your dog or dogs in general?

☆ If you use the same word every time you want your dog to perform the behavior, he will quickly associate that cue with the behavior. If, however, you are changing the cue or speaking in complicated sentences instead of one-word commands, the association will take some guesswork on the dog's part. Also, repetition can gum up your dog's understanding of the command. For example: "Fluffy, *come, come* Fluffy, *come, come,* Fluffy *come* . . ." can produce a dog who tunes you out or only comes after several commands, which can be dangerous for your *come* command

and irritating for *sits* or *downs*. There are no magic training words—the magic comes in the form of conditioning. The cue word becomes meaningful because the rewarded behavior is reliably associated with it. The result will be that *sit* means butt on the floor on Monday, Tuesday, Wednesday, and so on.

☆ If you are good at always praising before you deliver the treat, when your dog performs the requested behavior he will want to do it because of the treat. By praising before treating, you are classically conditioning your praise to have the same importance for your dog as the treat. This changes the wiring of your dog's brain so when you say, "Good boy," the neurons that process the sound of "good boy" and the neurons that process "Yeah, treat," always activate at the same time. When this connection is solidified, you can begin to fade out the treat.

  » WARNING: Never go cold turkey when fading treats. Only fading slowly will allow us to eliminate the treats entirely but still keep the useful associations.

☆ If the task you are asking your dog to do is difficult because of who your dog is, you may want to select an easier task, or find a way to make the task easier in the early stages of training. For example, if you're asking your herding dog to ignore your baby moving right in front of him, instead of asking the dog to *come*, you might want to let the dog keep his eyes on the child but lock him in place with a *down* or a *sit* command. Herding dogs are frequently happier when they are allowed to keep an eye on the movement around them. You need to know your dog's strengths and weaknesses and take the "should" out of your training. When you ask for something your dog is happy to do or

TRAINING TIPS

can physically do better, he will be more likely to comply with your request and you can build from there. If you had all the time in the world to train your dog, you could work on the tough stuff, but with the complications of a busy household with kids and dogs—take what will work and add on to that when you have more time.

★ **Which is faster, *luring* or *shaping*?** This is an ongoing debate in the training community. Generally, I will often **lure** at the beginning of teaching some commands and then shape to proof the command. But there are other commands that I will only shape. When training dogs around kids, **luring** will probably be faster. Although it may result in some messy commands, it doesn't matter how goofy it looks as long as you are getting what you need.

☆ *Luring* is usually done with a treat in your hand, which is resting at the dog's nose. It works like a magnet, with your dog's nose representing the piece of metal, and your hand with the treat acting as the magnet. There is also distance *luring*—for example, the *go sniff* command is a distance *lure*.

An example of *luring* would go like this: You want your dog to lie *down,* so you take some treats and close them up in your fist. Rest your fist on your dog's nose, and once she is sniffing eagerly at your hand, slowly lower your fist to the floor directly below her nose. As her nose follows your hand and starts to poke your fist on the floor as if to say, "What do I have to do to get the treat?" you leave your hand on the floor—don't move it until the dog begins to bring her front legs down, and then you might move your hand toward the dog just a bit, or you might not, depending on how easily she is moving into the *down*. Once she is all *down*—elbows and hind-end on the floor—you praise her and open your hand, giving her the jackpot. After she does this a few times, you can add in the verbal command right before the *luring* motion. Over time you will take the treats out of your hand and continue the luring motion without the treat if you want to develop a hand signal to go along with the verbal command.

☆ Shaping takes much more time in some cases and is faster in others. When shaping, we wait for the dog to perform the desired behavior and then praise him and reward him. If the desired behavior is something the dog does often, shaping is quick. But if the behavior is something the dog would never think to do, shaping could be a slower process. For example, if your dog is excited around your baby and you want him to lie *down*, he may be too excited to think of that, so *luring* will help him to do the behavior you want. But if your dog naturally lies down next to you when you read to your child, then shaping would work out well because all you have to do is praise and reward the naturally occurring *down*. Once you see your dog about to perform the desired behavior, quickly say the command as he is initiating the behavior. Over time, he will associate the command with the behavior and voilà—a behavior is shaped.

★ How do you exercise baby, dog, and yourself? This answer is predicated on mutual enjoyment of the same activities. If you love walking with your dog, then bring the baby and if the dog has good *loose-leash walking* skills (see below for details), then every one gets out and exercised. If you love grabbing and tossing gooey tennis balls or deflated soccer balls, then fetch is the game for you and your dog (see below for details).

TRAINING TIPS

★ *Loose-leash walking* position means that as you walk, your dog is walking with a loose (wiggly) leash near your side but not in heel position. Generally, your dog should be somewhere in a three-foot semicircle next to you—typically on the left—a little in front or behind is fine. Your dog has a peripheral vision of 250 degrees, so he can still keep an eye on you for directions if he is a little ahead of you.

Initially, your dog would start learning this type of walking without the stroller in front of you or the baby walking beside you. Once he is good at *loose-leash walking*, then it will be time to introduce the stroller into the mix. I like to hold the leash loop in my right hand and then lay a portion of the leash across the top of the stroller handle, holding the stroller handle and the leash simultaneously with both hands, allowing me to steer with two hands and have two hands on the leash, too. This position gives me a little more stability and keeps the leash from tangling up in the stroller.

If your dog pulls when on leash, then a group walk will require two parents—one walking the dog and the other walking the baby. This exercise is well worth it for you and your baby, and for the relationship between your dog and your baby. Most dogs love going out for walks, so these walks would mean that every time your dog goes out with you and your baby, he will be associating great outings with your child, and the positive link will continue to strengthen their relationship.

My four favorite exercises for teaching *loose-leash walking* are Watch Me Walking, Crazy Ivans, and Incremental Sits, with the occasional need to do some Shameless *Luring*.

☆ **Watch Me Walking:** In this exercise, we reinforce our dog's good behavior with praise, treats, and more movement each and every time he looks at us before we start walking. We are turning the dog looking at us into the only reason our human feet can move. If your dog is looking at you, you walk. But if he is not looking at you, your feet don't budge (unless you are in the middle of a street). It is not unlike a doggie version of the children's game Red Light, Green Light. If your dog is locked on something—another dog, a squirrel, or a skunk—don't wait for him to look at you. Instead, turn and walk in the other direction, and then resume working the Watch Me Walking exercise when your dog is no longer stuck on the distraction.

☆ **Crazy Ivans:** For this exercise, we use body movement as our greatest attention-getting device. Crazy Ivans are designed to randomize the walking and keep your dog watching you every step of the way. While walking, you will change directions for no apparent reason, giving your dog a cue before turning ("with me" or "turning") and then providing huge praise when your dog comes along. Sometimes you will treat and reward and sometimes the movement and the joy of the game will reinforce the dog. (I stole the name of this game from *The Hunt for Red October*.)

☆ **Incremental Sits:** This exercise is tedious but very effective. Stick with it, and it will pay off. Begin with one step and ask for a *sit*, next take two steps and ask for a *sit*, then take three steps and ask for a *sit*, then four steps, and keep going from there. If your dog ever gets out of *loose-leash walking* position, return to one step and begin the process again. At first, rewards must be consistent with each *sit*; later they can be given randomly for both walking and sitting.

☆ **Shameless *Luring*:** When you and your dog need to walk together through a highly distracting situation, use this technique to glue your dog's attention to your hand (filled with treats). Like all the rest of these exercises, it will need to be practiced, and eventually it will teach your dog that following your hand, even without the treats, is valuable. It works best for dogs whose nose and mouth are easy to reach as you walk. Simply take a good number of stinky dog treats and close them in your left hand. Rest your hand on your dog's nose and walk. We are playing the magnet game again, but this time while walking.

★ **Fetch** is one of the most common games people think of when they think of dogs. It is also one of the games they give up on easily, because many dogs do not know how to play this game intuitively. Even if your dog already plays fetch, it is worth reading below to build the baby-friendly fetch.

☆ The first step to fetch is the *drop it* command. Hand your dog something to take in his mouth. Ask him to *drop it* for payment. The payment can be a food reward or another toy. It is imperative in the first step that your dog drop the item at your feet or close by you, allowing you to teach him to bring it back more easily later on.

☆ Once he is happily dropping the toy at your feet, hand him the toy and take a step away from him—maybe a foot. Ask for the *drop it* and hold out your hand to show the reward waiting for him. Hopefully, he will approach with the toy and drop it next to your hand for the treat. If he does not, go back to step one and repeat a few more times.

☆ Once step two is working well and your dog is happily bringing the toy to you from a foot away, you can slowly begin to increase the distance. Remember, some dogs will get fetch right off the bat and be able to bring the toy to you from a long distance quickly. Other dogs will look at you as if to say, "You threw it; you go get it." Not all dogs are born retrievers—even some retrievers aren't—but they can all learn this game. When your dog is good at this and you are building more distance between you and your dog, it will be time to add the *come* command. Once your dog reaches you, ask for *drop it*.

☆ Fine-tuning fetch for baby, toddler, or older children means the dog will bring the object back and drop it at your child's feet or in his or her lap in the stroller. Then you reward the dog. Although the dog and child are part of the play, the parents refocus the dog back to themselves after the toy is dropped. This refocus keeps the dog from mouthing or jumping on the child in an attempt to move the play along, and it allows older kids to have time to pick up the ball or toy to throw it without the dog repossessing the toy before the child can pick it up. Many dogs will take advantage of the clumsy toddler and take back the toy before the child gets it. This could turn into a new unfortunate game of keep away. It can also cause the child to become afraid of the dog because teeth are usually involved in getting the toy.

★ **When will you be able to let your dog and baby play together?** It is not about a predetermined age. It depends on your dog, your child, and the space where they play.

☆ If you answer yes to any of the following questions, you will need to remain actively involved in play between your dog and your child:

» Does your dog show any fear around your child?

TRAINING TIPS

- Does your dog flinch or run away when your child plays with him or reaches out for him?

- Does your dog crouch down and look like what most people call submissive? (This is a fearful stance and is not as good as most people think.)

» Does your dog bark at your child when he or she is running or playing silly movement-oriented games—jumping, dancing, and so on? (This barking can mean your dog is excited or it could mean these things worry or scare your dog. Since we cannot ask the dog, we should err on the side of caution in the early stages and review the basics of DS/CC.)

» Is your dog still mouthy when he plays with you or anyone?

☆ If you answered no to the questions above and answer yes to the following questions, you can begin to allow your child and dog to play together with you always nearby, but not actively involved.

» Does your dog actively want to be with your child? (This is often demonstrated by your dog hanging out on the other side of the gate or following you and the baby around the house, and gently interacting when baby is having belly time, lying on your lap, or playing with you in the area.)

» Has your child demonstrated that he or she can pet the dog gently? Is your baby not hitting the dog when frustrated, to see what happens, or because he or she doesn't have good motor skills yet?

» Does your dog enjoy your child petting him?

» Does your dog have a reliable *come* so you can call him out of play at the slightest inkling of trouble? (It is often easier to get the dog out than to get a young child to follow rules. Remember, "When in doubt—get the dog out.")

» Does the space where they will be playing allow for an easy out for the dog? (It is important to remember that your dog needs more room than the average person to feel comfortable. He will be more stressed as the area of play gets tighter, for example, if furniture is blocking exits or open play areas. The best play area would be wide open, with a couple of exits for the dog if he feels the play is getting to be too much and wants to withdraw.)

CHAPTER TWELVE

Beware the Rise of the TODDLER

....

Typically, sometime after the first birthday most babies go from tottering individual steps to that uniquely human form of locomotion—full-blown, two-legged walking. This is a happy day for most parents. However, I am sure that if dogs had a storytelling method to transfer knowledge from one generation to the next—like a canine troubadour—they would sing about the legend of the *toddler*, with appropriately ominous music.

He came to us small and smelly—we loved him.
He grew quickly by bones too many to count, and now he chases, grabs, and hits us.
Beware the toddler: we love him but he is capricious.

From the dog's perspective, the toddler is completely unpredictable. At one moment he's great fun and the next moment really scary (some adults feel this way, too). This developmental stage is when I often get the call from many parents, when the baby begins walking, grabbing, and throwing things or having tantrums. If everything has been going well up to this point, dogs are often surprised and scared when their toddler begins to roam the house and beelines for them with hands out like pincers from the arcade Claw Machine. If the dog can get away, he often will. If not, some will be tolerant and others will defend themselves with a growl, snap, or bite.

This is also the time when children are starting to figure out they have some effect on the world around them. Testing things like, "If I drop this spoon, someone, usually my parents, will pick it up—over and over." And if kids have a dog in their lives they may quickly realize, "Hey if I drop this toy, the dog picks it up and my parents chase the dog around until the dog earns enough to release it . . . cool!" When I saw Indy looking back at us as if to say, "I know you don't want me to do this, but I'm gonna anyway. Whatcha gonna do about it?" I knew he would apply this approach with the rules about the dogs, too.

One of the trickier elements of training dogs and kids together is we cannot explain to the dog that if she would just ignore the child's unwanted behaviors, these behaviors will usually extinguish themselves. Instead, the dog will almost always respond to the child—good or bad—which means the dog consistently reinforces our child's behavior—good or bad.

Every time Indy threw his toys, we could ignore it or take the toy away, but Pinball would always be there ready and willing to run off with it, encouraging Indy to throw more. As Indy's toys became more complicated, with more pieces like puzzles, blocks, and crayons, Indy's favorite fling-the-toy-at-Pinball game became more complicated because the pieces were smaller, more numerous, and more easily swallowed by the relentless canine eating machine. Pinball could no longer be within Indy's throwing range. Instead, we had to step back to a higher level of management and put an extra space called no-dogs-land between Indy and Pinball. If Indy were in the play yard in the living room, then Pinball had to be on the other side of the gates in the kitchen area. If Indy had free reign of the living room, Pinball had to be on the other side of the second set of baby gates separating the two halves of the house, leaving the whole empty kitchen between him and Indy. I felt like this separation was a setback, but reminded myself that I knew the day would come when Indy had even more mobility and many things would have to change.

These new rules would be in effect until we got the throwing or the guarding under control—whichever came first. However, the new rules did not need to be implemented upstairs. Pinball behaved better outside the upstairs play yard, even though we had the same configuration of equipment and the same baby toys. The different locations produced different behaviors. This varied behavior is both a testament to dogs' tendencies to have unique sets of behaviors for different environments and a cautionary tale to remember dogs don't generalize well. Just because Pinball was okay giving up Indy's toys upstairs didn't mean it would translate to downstairs. Because I knew why, it didn't frustrate me and it allowed me to make the necessary changes downstairs without giving it a second thought.

Indy, following the baby manual that all kids seem to receive upon being born, was doing a good job of stabilizing himself on his (back) legs. Because of the gates and the configuration of our house, Indy had the ability to grab onto something to steady himself regardless of where he was in the living room, and if he fell there were usually dog pillows to break his fall.

One of Indy's favorite early discoveries was the adventure of climbing up the two layers of dog pillows in front of Boo's chair. The pillows were there to give Boo a helping paw up to his favorite chair, but they allowed Indy to have the same advantage getting up there. Indy enjoyed scrambling up the pillow mountain to the expansive chair and either hanging out with Boo, or sliding back down so he could climb back up and slide down over and over. Sometimes Indy hung out with Boo in a calm and orderly fashion. But sometimes Indy would hold onto the arm of the chair and bounce around as if on a trampoline, with no regard for Boo right next to him. I had to intervene when that happened lest Indy fall off (probably headfirst) and because it wasn't safe for Boo, who couldn't see to get out of the way and was likely to get bounced on. Boo's tolerance at these times was almost saintly.

Boo's patience with Indy allowed him the most freedom and vice versa. But there were more and more occasions when it was clear Boo was trying to get away from Indy, who would occasionally chase him through the living room. These freedoms that Boo and Indy shared ended one day when I stepped out of the living room into the kitchen to start preparing the dogs' dinner. Hearing the sounds of the bowls, Boo got up from his chair to make his way to his feeding station and Indy, who had been playing in the living room, chased Boo between the highchair and the wall. Boo couldn't find his way out from the corner and began yelping when Indy grabbed the fur on his shoulder as if he were trying to mount a horse bareback. Luckily, the living room is adjacent to the kitchen so I could get there quickly to intervene. Boo's forgiving nature and love of children probably saved Indy from at least a snap that day. If it had been Pinball or Porthos, we would have had a very different outcome. In this instance, all I had to do was step between Indy and Boo, escort Boo out of the corner, put Indy into his play yard, and feed the dogs to get all commotion under control.

Even though Boo was no threat to Indy in that moment, I couldn't let that one instance lead me to the conclusion that

Boo would always be okay no matter what Indy did. That kind of assumption often leads to trouble. Instead, the lesson I took was, "Things have changed. The toddler has risen." I knew that even if certain things had worked in the past, Indy's developmental changes would require me to alter my management strategies to match his level of activity—for all the dogs, not just Pinball anymore. The result was a new and improved plan for Boo when Indy was roaming around the living room—we called it the Boo fortress-of-solitude. It was really just moving the dog pillows from in front of Boo's chair and stacking them on top of the ottoman. This way, Indy couldn't climb up anymore and Boo couldn't get down without our help. This management left us time to secure the toddler before Boo got off the chair, allowing Boo to remain in the living room while Indy was free to roam and explore—for the time being anyway.

Porthos was the only dog in our house not to encounter the toddler insult—he had avoided being poked and pinched or conked on the head with a flying toy. This was mostly because his approach to anything that troubled him was to go to another room. The only change that had to be made for Porthos as Indy became more nomadic was to support his choice to leave the situations and sometimes suggest he go before he would have normally exited—he was happy to comply. The rise of the toddler was made much easier for all the dogs because they were used to the safety net of the gates. Household management didn't come as a shocking out-of-the-blue change because it had already been built into our daily routines.

I can think of two clients who did great jobs of building behaviors for their dogs around their new babies yet forgot the simple premise that maybe their dogs wouldn't want to be around their toddlers quite as much they did. In the case of the first client, there was no physical management in place when the twenty-pound little girl started crawling over the ninety-pound lab-mix. The parents were shocked when their dog growled at her. Luckily, they called me and we reviewed factors like the body language signals the dog was giving that said, "Please let me be—I'm snoozing," and the need for a safe spot for the dog to go where the little girl couldn't get to him. But, most important, we addressed their need to understand that the dog was not aggressive just because he didn't want to be crawled on. He just needed his adult humans to step up and keep him safe while the baby was developing better skills around him.

In the second case, I had known little Queenie since she was a twelve-week-old puppy and had worked with her and her owner through some issues regarding fear of strangers. As a result, Queenie and her owner were well versed in desensitizing and counter-conditioning exercises and when to allow Queenie space away from strangers. Queenie's owner, Nina, loved her dog with a great passion and was determined to keep her in spite of discouraging opinions from family and friends regarding Queenie's seemingly aggressive behaviors. Nina and her husband did everything right in terms of including Queenie in all the things they could with their newborn son, like reading time and dinnertime. When Nina emailed me after Queenie had growled at her son, she was heartbroken and terrified that she would have to rehome or euthanize Queenie, knowing that she (like Pinball) would not be a dog easily rehomed. I, too, was worried at first until I arrived at the home and saw that they had done so many things right. There were several baby gates around the house, Nina encouraged happy baby-dog time, and Queenie still had her basic commands in place after eight years. It was fairly easy to adjust the situation so Queenie could have an escape route from the grasping hands of Nina's son, who apparently loved Queenie as much as his mama did, just without the adult understanding of how and when to show it. Almost a year and a half later, Queenie and her little boy were still doing well together.

In both cases the owners had done enough training and preparation for the baby-dog situation when they became pregnant that things never got way out of hand. They felt comfortable contacting me when things went off the rails as their toddlers started pushing the limitations of their dog's tolerance levels. For many parents who have not had any baby-dog issues until their baby became a toddler, when they find themselves faced with a dog who is growling at their child, panic often sets in. If there has been no training or management put into place up to this point, that panic can often result in a knee-jerk reaction on the parent's part. It can never be repeated enough that a growling dog needs our help to defuse the fearful elements of the situation, and it is never too late to set up the kind of training, management, and guidance that will help your dog stay with the family she loves while you keep your baby safe.

Whenever I doubted my household policies in terms of managing Pinball, Boo, and Porthos around Indy, I reminded myself of the number of colleagues who told me how they had a beloved dog when they became a parent but had to give the dog up when he or she growled at the baby. It was almost as if they were trying to prepare me for what was to come. I reminded myself of the number of dogs who are relinquished to shelters every year because their family has a new baby. I was going to move heaven and earth to be sure this was not our fate, and, as anticipated, the rise of the toddler was putting all my strategies to the ultimate test.

• • •

Training Tips You Can Try at Home:

★ What is it about toddlers that gets to so many dogs?
★ How can we make the toddler-trigger easier for
   our dogs?
★ Escape routes
★ Your dog has growled, now what?

★ What is it about toddlers that gets to so many dogs?

This question should be asked more often. But because many people feel their good dog can or should withstand anything their child has to throw at her (literally and figuratively), the question is not asked, and without questions there can be no help in the form of answers.

I knew even before having a toddler that they are bundles of energy with quick, unsteady bursts of movement. The literature about toddlers is filled with buzzwords that should scare the dickens out of anyone approaching this milestone: defiance, pitching fits, tantrums, and getting into everything. From the dog's perspective many, if not all, of those can be difficult to process.

☆ Quick, unsteady movements are triggers for your dog's predatory or flight instincts.

> » Dogs have been honed by nature to react to quick movements for survival. Such movements signal that their dinner awaits. Your dog may not be looking at your toddler as a prey animal, but they are still programmed to chase anything that moves quickly and erratically. Think squirrels, bunnies, and even darting deer, and then ask if your toddler's play movements resemble any of these animals. In

this stage your toddler is triggering a very primal instinct in your dog. Some dogs learn not to chase the child, but they are in the minority. Most homes with toddlers and dogs report multiple nippings of ankles, pants legs, and hands as children move through the house.

» The flip side of this instinct is the flight instinct that arises when the child chases the dog. Chasing can result in a type of play for your dog that mimics survival behavior. But if the game goes from play to something that feels like real survival for your dog, it can result in your dog feeling the need to defend herself, much like my client's Schipperke in the beginning of this book who was chased by her toddler with the toy lawn mower.

☆ **Defiance, getting into everything, pitching fits, and tantrums all come with a host of scary possibilities from your dog's perspective.**

» Screaming tantrums can be loud. Pinball came running every time I combed Indy's hair and Indy's screaming cut through the house like a band saw. Perhaps Pinball was concerned, but that didn't mean he would make the right decisions about how to handle his concern.

» Pitching fits involves arms flailing and anything nearby potentially flying across the room. If Indy was not happy about a diaper change that interrupted his play, every diaper product within reach was a potential projectile to punctuate his fit. More than once, Pinball ended up covered in the flying baby powder, but shook it off as he made a hasty retreat. If he could not retreat, he would be pushed to defend himself.

» Defiance usually brings a tone, or sometimes a form of toddler passive resistance, accompanied by flying items. For example, one day as we were leaving for day care, Pinball picked up a toy I thought had been put away. When

I asked Pinball to *drop it*, he went to his usual spot. But because Indy and I were on our way out, we were both standing next to the pillow to deliver the treat, and Indy wanted to move toward Pinball. When I said no, he went into his passive resistance and fell flat on the floor. All that pushed Pinball's stress buttons and he wouldn't drop the toy as usual. This simple act of defiance from Indy was enough for Pinball to regress to a panicked state about the stolen toy.

A toddler's passive resistance position on the floor can also leave him or her at risk for being injured by the dog—being stepped on, mouthed, or worse. In these instances, I ask Pinball for a *down* because that is his best holding position.

★ How can we make the toddler-trigger easier for our dogs?

☆ The predatory instinct is hard to stop—after all, nature engineers very powerful mechanisms. However, luckily for us, a piece of that predatory instinct is the dog's food drive. We can use that to help our dogs move away from zany toddler movements.

» The *go sniff* command involving tossed treats is probably the best option to interrupt toddler chasing. Most dogs love the *go sniff* game, but if they love chasing the toddler more, you might need to use a higher value treat, like cheese, for tossing instead of standard treats.

» Timing is critical. As the toddler moves in one direction, toss the treats/cheese with the command *go sniff* in the other direction. This teaches the dog to go away from the running toddler instead of after him or her. It also lets the toddler play whatever game is going on while keeping you (not your toddler) as the main focus in the game for your dog. After one or two *go sniffs*, the dog can be sent to the other side of a baby gate to relax while your child continues the human version of puppy zoomies (a.k.a. frenetic random activity periods, or FRAPs).

» This game is more difficult in a yard where it is easier for the dog and child to quickly put distance between themselves and the parent, making it problematic for the parent to remain between the child and dog. For our backyard baby-dog adventures I use leashes.

For walks in the woods, Pinball wears his harness and leash and Indy wears his monkey backpack with leash. I can keep each of them where I want them and manage their interactions. Indy is much faster than I am. His monkey allows me to relax and let him go, knowing that he can only go so far. This works everywhere he wants to run—woods, mall, sidewalks, zoo.

When they are both in the fenced area of the yard, I have Indy on the monkey leash to keep him from getting to Pinball, who is running free. In the yard all Pinball wants is to run and be chased—but not caught. This format is kind of unusual, but it works well and all of us are happy with it.

★ **Escape routes** employ the commands I have spoken about previously in Chapters Five and Nine, like *go sniff* and **touch**, but formalizes where the dog goes with those commands and how. We have to keep the dog's path clear so she can always rely on being able to get out via that route. For example, Queenie needed a pathway that would allow her to move through the family room to the hallway past Nina's son. It was easy to build because she knew the *go sniff* command, so all we were doing was adding to that by teaching Queenie the *out you go* command, which means "leave the room completely via a specific path."

☆ When setting up a pathway, look for the route that will be easiest for the dog and will most likely not have your child in the way. Things to consider when setting up an escape route are people, furniture, scary baby toys, and floor surfaces.

» Some dogs will not want to pass by a person near a doorway and will be reluctant to move at the speed you may need them to pass people. Pick a route that is not a hangout space for guests.

» Some dogs do not like going under tables or through narrow passageways between furniture or scary baby toys. Be sure the route will not be obstructed by moved furniture or toys.

» Some dogs are not comfortable on all floor surfaces—the more slippery the surface, the harder it is for some. These surfaces may be something they manage regularly, but when they are stressed or feel at risk they will be less likely to want to be on a surface that makes them ill at ease. Be mindful of your dog's comfort on a variety of surfaces and pick a route that takes them over the household terrain they prefer.

★ Your dog has growled. Now what?

☆ The first thing is to use a preconditioned escape route to get the dog out, or employ one of the increase distance commands like *go sniff, touch,* or *come* to put space between your dog and your child.

☆ Secure the dog in another room, behind a gate, or in a crate.

☆ Take a breath and console your child if need be.

☆ Assess. Your dog growling at your child is a wake-up call that lets let you know your dog has a problem with something. It is time to figure out what that is and ask if it can be safely fixed.

TRAINING TIPS

☆ Here are a few questions to help determine what made your dog growl.

» Is your baby new to the home and a totally new experience for your dog?

» Was your child reaching for your dog when the dog was asleep?

» Could your dog be in pain because of a long hike, a misstep when jumping, age, or other factors?

It is easy for us not to be aware when our dogs are in pain. Typically, we become aware of their pain only when it is so bad that it inhibits their movement, like limping, or they begin to vocalize, like whining. At that point, they are in a great deal of pain.

» Was your toddler chasing the dog into a corner where he felt trapped?

» Was the child simply petting the dog and then the petting turned into fur grabbing, ear tugging, pinching, or eye poking?

» Was your child trying to hug or hugging your dog?

Dogs are not comfortable with most people hugging them. The act of putting front legs around another dog and holding on is not a polite or safe thing to do in the dog's world, so when a human does it, it is pretty scary for them. Many dogs get used to it from their favorite person but not the "outsiders" in their lives, and until your child has earned your dog's trust, he or she will be one of the outsiders.

» Did your dog have a bone or another resource and thought the child was too close?

☆ Once we know what caused the dog to growl, we can begin to manage future situations. In some cases, that means teaching the child what is appropriate to do around and to the dog. In other cases, it will mean managing the dog so he is in another room when your child is in a more rambunctious play mood or when your dog has a resource that is important to him. And sometimes, it will be desensitizing and counter-conditioning the dog to the child because your dog is afraid of or doesn't like kids.

☆ "But I want my toddler to be able to do anything to the dog," is like saying, "I want my toddler to play safely in the street without my having to worry about cars."

A study by the Institute of Transportation Engineers has shown us that children develop adult skills slowly and not all at once. A young child who seems mature and tells you that he or she understands to look both ways will still not be able to safely judge the gaps between cars or the actual distance of a vehicle. I am waiting and hoping for similar research into a young child's ability to read dog body language and accurately judge the dog's safety. But for now, I suggest we take the same precautions we do to protect small children in traffic and apply them to children and dogs.

There are times and places when playing in the street is fun and safe. There are ages that are better suited to judge that. Until then, as we are waiting for the perfect combination of a safe street and good judgment, we need to manage and guide our children. We need to view the growl from a dog as we would the honk of a horn from a driver letting us know our child is in harm's way.

CHAPTER THIRTEEN

Just When You Think You Are Safe

W hy things always seem to go wrong for Pinball in October is a question that will probably stay with me forever.

When Lawrence and I were on the adoption waiting list, we planned our lives as normally as we could. One of those plans was a cruise we booked ten months before Indy was born. We were overjoyed to have to postpone that trip because it coincided with Indy's due date, and were lucky Lawrence had taken the cruise insurance. Almost a year after Indy's arrival, we realized we had to use the credit for that trip or lose it. After Lawrence confirmed that his parents would sit both Indy and our animals, we booked the last cruise available—an early October cruise to Bermuda. We had some concerns about the trip being through hurricane territory at the height of hurricane season. Little did we know that was the least of our worries.

It's a difficult thing to explain to friends and family that your cute, little puppy developed major behavioral issues around twenty-one months and is now a dog that can pose some risks.

Trying to anticipate all the potential pitfalls that could happen during our trip, I asked my in-laws to do a dry run and spend the night with Indy and the dogs while we stayed at a nearby hotel so we could come home quickly if there were any problems. This dry run would offer me insight into what specific issues might crop up for my in-laws so I could work on those before the actual trip when there would be no possibility of us coming home in an emergency. My warnings about Pinball were downplayed when Lawrence reminded me that Pinball loves my in-laws, and Lawrence's parents didn't see the need for the dry run because they had sat for him before with no issues.

Unfortunately, since the last time much had changed in the house and in Pinball's life. With a dry run off the table, I lobbied for a weekend visit with us there to give me the opportunity to run Lawrence's parents through Pinball's behavioral needs and Porthos's insulin delivery because the two issues were inextricably linked. If Porthos wasn't feeling well, then Pinball would become anxious, and when Pinball was anxious he guarded more and was more likely to bite if anyone tried to take a stolen item from him—even me. Then there was the possibility of one of Porthos's full-blown OCD episodes, during which multiple additional medicines, including injections, were necessary. I was told I was being a pessimist (not a wholly inaccurate statement), but just because you're a pessimist doesn't mean things won't go wrong.

With no option for a weekend visit, I asked if Lawrence's parents could come out for a day so I could show them a few tricks for the resource guarding and the insulin delivery. The pessimist in me was validated when Lawrence looked at me and said, "I just figured someone would be dropping by to give Porthos his shots."

"Who did you think would be coming by twice a day to do this?" was my response, punctuated by a few expletives. Both of

us needed a vacation, and we both enjoyed the cruises we had
been on in the past, but I was pretty much getting ready to send
Lawrence alone.

I was able to recruit Karen, a dog walker I knew through
a few of my clients, to come by twice a day for Porthos's injections. She had experience with insulin and she and I had worked
together with clients' dogs, so I trusted her to be able to handle our crew. I had her come out a couple of times to let her get
to know the gang, especially Pinball. They all seemed to enjoy
her and she felt comfortable with them. I felt a little better, but
still had misgivings about Pinball's guarding erupting into a bite
during my in-laws' stay.

My in-laws came out the night before we were to leave and
I tried to give them the CliffsNotes version of everything they
would need. I typed up notes on each dog and the dozen pages
were welcomed like a tax audit. They balked at having Karen
come over for Porthos's insulin, saying, "How hard can it be?"

I tried to explain that an inexact dosage could kill Porthos
and they didn't have direct experience with diabetes, so I held
firm on Karen being the only one to give the injections. When it
came to Pinball's resource guarding, I said unequivocally, "If he
gets something, just let him have it."

It was the lesser of all the evils to have him destroy something or make himself sick than to come home to another bite
on his record. I also showed them how they could use the trail of
treats away from the object if what he had was something they
really needed to get back. I got the sense that my instructions
were causing annoyance, as if I were suggesting they were not
competent to keep our son safe. In reality I was not as worried
about Indy as I was about them.

With many misgivings (on my part only) we left for our trip
and had a lovely relaxing time. We received email reports from

Lawrence's parents every couple of days telling us that all was well and everyone was doing fine. Upon our return, my in-laws were eager to leave after they spent time with Lawrence and Indy outside while I said hello to the dogs. My Spidey-sense was on full alert, telling me something was wrong.

No sooner had Lawrence and I waved his parents out of the driveway than two weeks of continuous arguing over Pinball's life began. Lawrence told me Pinball had bitten both his parents when they tried to "beat him to something he had stolen." Having warned everyone and directed them to "let Pinball have it," only to be ignored, I didn't feel Pinball should have to pay with his life. I was unhappy that I was not told face-to-face about these bites so I could get accurate information to determine their nature and Pinball's level of culpability. I was angry with Lawrence that instead of securing Karen when we made the initial plans for the trip, I was told my in-laws would be fine and I was just being a worrywart. And I was livid that my dog had injured my in-laws and it had all been preventable. I spoke with Karen and she had had no problems with any of the dogs and said they were lovely.

Our arguments over Pinball were complicated and more like a tournament than a single fight. We went over the issues, through the issues, around the issues, and back over them again and again. Lawrence's position was aligned with his parents, lobbying to euthanize Pinball because they felt he was dangerous. I countered that Lawrence had taken that position with Porthos on each occasion when he had injured an animal in the house—yet Porthos was a valued, loved, and trusted member of our house (with the right management).

My point for Pinball was the same as it had been with Porthos: We were the ones who needed to understand the situation and take the necessary steps to make the dog behaviorally safe. If those steps were not taken, then we could not blame the dog.

But if we did take those steps and the dog still could not be made safe, then the conversation could return to euthanasia. I reminded Lawrence of all the good work Pinball did with many of my clients and the fact that while he ultimately made the choice to bite, *we* set him up for that failure. Lawrence and I continued our arguing tournament, going through rounds such as how it would crush Indy to have Pinball gone, and what would we do if Pinball bit Indy, and then back to management strategies—were they enough and what if they failed—round after round.

Each of us assessed what risks we were setting Indy up to face. We even had a list comparing the dogs to other dangers he would face in life and around our house, such as using our fireplace, learning to drive, or playing a concussion-prone sport. Ultimately, we had to ask what could we control, what could we expect a toddler to know or process, and what were the dangers that could be reliably managed.

We concluded several things: our physical management and reliable verbal commands were in place, if we kept Pinball we would need more caretakers like Karen, and it would be almost impossible to responsibly rehome Pinball. This left us with only two options: keeping and working with him, or euthanizing Pinball.

Another round of up-training for Pinball was set into motion. "Up-training" is a higher level of proofing that usually involves new skills to offset new challenges. I enlisted Karen to come over, on a monthly basis at first, to allow the dogs to remain comfortable with her and vice versa. I talked to Pinball's veterinarian and we upped his Prozac to the maximum dose, and added some amino acid supplements to reduce his anxiety and owner-directed aggression. I continued to train control behaviors to lock Pinball *down* quickly with a verbal command, or move him with a word or hand signal. I also continued to build the relationship between

Pinball and Indy by keeping Pinball involved in as much of that little boy's life as I could, while keeping Indy at arm's length (or, in this case, Pinball's jump length).

About two weeks after we returned from the cruise, I was off again for the annual Association of Professional Dog Trainers conference. I was bombarded with seminars, workshops, and unsolicited stories of dogs biting kids, or the horrors of resource guarding, and once again I was taking these presentations personally. But it forced me to take a dispassionate look at what I was doing by keeping Pinball in the house.

I worked in rescue and knew well how often we got the dogs people threw away, thinking someone else would be able to fix what they could not. I was not going to be that person. I had been there the day Pinball was born; he was the only dog I had ever had whom I had known from birth. Between that and the emotional trauma we went through with his litter's parvovirus and Callie's death, I was too emotionally invested in this funny little dog. I had to find a way to help Pinball do better and keep Indy safe.

People will often scratch their heads in amazement over what dog-folk will go through for their dogs, asking, "Is that normal?"

I have clients who live with dogs far more dangerous than Pinball, but they make accommodations for them. Some clients spend almost $600 a month for doggie day care, while others have built additions onto their homes for various dogs' needs, or installed outdoor kennels for their dogs to go into when they have company. The list of things we dog lovers will do is limitless. But in everything, including dog ownership, there is no normal. In fact, the argument could be made that for the dog trainer, abnormal is the norm. The homes of most dog trainers, especially those of us who work with rescues, are often a haven for the dogs who need a little more help than the average dog.

We are often drawn to the hard-luck cases that can present more challenging behaviors, and often we are the only ones willing to take them.

Waiting for my flight back to New York from Spokane, I thought about other professionals whose work might generate lifestyles that others don't consider normal or safe. No one balks at police officers who keep their service weapons at home with small children. The officers are taught how to manage their guns by locking the guns and ammunition up separately. It is becoming more and more common for contractors and other tradespeople to sometimes bring their children onto a job site with all the dangers lurking there. Management and training keep these kids safe. As professionals, we accept these risks and realize we, as the parents, have to take steps to keep our children safe around these dangers. The police officer doesn't quit her job when she has children—she gets a gun safe. The contractor doesn't get rid of her business when she has to take care of children—she gets a hard hat for her child.

There is no such thing as normal across the board. There is only the individual normal that each of us creates, just as we create our families. In *our* home normal is a dog who 98 percent of the time is smart, funny, and affectionate but who, during the 2 percent, has to be managed and watched to prevent him from doing harm.

Two days after I returned from the conference, Pinball and I were working with a client whose dog was terrified of me unless Pinball was there. Pinball performed beautifully with the dog and his owners. They told me, "We love Pinball."

I was starting to feel a little better and Halloween a couple of days later helped buoy all our spirits even more. The joy that always came with Halloween was a welcome change from the previous few weeks. It was that much more fun because we took

Indy to his Auntie Jill and Linda's for his first trick-or-treating in an extremely cute monster costume—that was even cuter because it was a little too big for him and kept falling over half his face.

Theirs is a quaint family neighborhood with kids and dogs in almost every house. While we adults had a good time seeing all the kids and enjoying all of Indy's candy, I was reminded how hard Halloween is for many dogs. From a dog's point of view, strangers keep coming to the house one after the other all night in weird and sometimes scary costumes. Jill and Linda had installed baby gates after our last visit so they, too, could relax when Indy visited. They were happy to have them for this year's trick-or-treaters because they were well positioned to keep their dogs at a comfortable distance from the scary costumed kids.

I was relieved that another tumultuous October had ended, but this time with a little candy-fueled joy.

• • •

Training Tips You Can Try at Home

★ Finding dog sitters or kennels
★ Halloween

★ **Finding dog sitters** or kennels is an emotional chore for most dog owners. There is a lot of worry and any number of potential returning-home horror stories, including sick dog, injured dog, or worse. There are issues surrounding house care, too. I had one client whose dog sitter was throwing pool parties without her permission. For complicated or difficult dogs, this chore has layers that make an already emotionally fraught task more difficult. Often those of us with complicated pets choose to take no trips at all, or we have to plan well in advance so we can find the right situation for our pets while we are away.

Currently the Internet is probably the most prolific source of dog sitters and kennels, but asking your friends, your veterinarian, and your dog trainer is essential to help you sort through the various listings online.

☆ One option is a dog sitter who stays at your house, or comes by multiple times each day. This person should be all of the following:

» Responsible, meaning you know he or she will do what you asked and not do things beyond your instructions (such as throwing pool parties).

» Willing to come by as many times as it takes before the trip to be sure the dog is comfortable with him or her. You will need to pay the dog walker for this "training," even if it involves nothing more than the dog walker chatting with you while treating the dogs as they acclimate to him or her.

» Able and willing to follow your instructions to the letter, including these basics:

- Feeding quantities and times.

- Medications given regularly at the appropriate intervals. (Obviously, Porthos was on the extreme end of complicated, but many dogs have health issues that require a good deal of attention to detail.)

- Walking and yard directions. (They have to be spelled out. For example, does your dog go out into a fenced yard, or does he need to be walked on a leash, or both? In addition, the equipment you normally use for walks needs to be indicated and demonstrated if the walker is not familiar with it.)

- Household rules, like *sit* and *wait* commands before feeding, furniture rules, and so on.

☆ We owners have responsibilities vis-à-vis the dog sitter that include the following:

» Advance notice so the sitter can secure his or her schedule.

» Willingness to pay the sitter to come by to get to know the animals and practice the household routines, which may need demonstrating.

» Friends as backup. In the event the dog sitter becomes ill, or has an emergency, it is important we provide contact information for our friends or family who can help in an emergency.

☆ Another option is kenneling. For many dogs, kennels are too stressful, and for others it is like going to camp. You have to know your dog and give it a trial run if you are unsure how your dog will do. The trial run would be a short stay for one or two nights to see how your dog does, with you still at home in case you need an emergency canine extraction.

» Dogs with difficult medical issues like Porthos's are hard to kennel because of the toll the stress takes on them, and the fact that not many kennels will take on dogs who require such precise medical management. When looking for a kennel, it is important to follow these guidelines:

- Visit the kennel personally and ask to see the facilities. I do not consider any kennel that won't give me a tour of where the dogs are housed.

- Things to look for include a clean and relatively quiet environment, an outdoor run attached to the inside kennel, an outdoor play area, specific exercise time with a staff member, and proximity to a veterinarian on call.

- I personally want a staff member on site throughout the night.

- Talk to the staff who will be taking care of the dogs and see if you are comfortable with them.

- Ask if you can call to check in on your dogs.

☆ Babysitters (family, friends, or professionals) and nannies are not technically employed to take care of your dogs, but sometimes that becomes part of their job description. Anytime folks are coming into your home to take care of your children, they will need to interact with your dogs unless you quarantine or kennel your dogs while they are there. When working with clients whose child care providers interact with their dogs regularly, I include them in the training as much as possible. Your child's nanny or babysitter should be apprised of and willing to comply with the following:

» How and when to use your dog's commands, and how and when to reinforce them.

» Appropriate ways to communicate and interact with the dog. I had one client whose housekeeper routinely hit her dog with cleaning tools. It didn't surprise me that this dog began to chase the housekeeper and bit her.

» Directions regarding when and how to allow the dog and children together.

» How to prevent your dog's unwanted behaviors, either by implementing training techniques or managing the dog.

★ **Halloween** is frequently not a happy time for many dogs, who are freaked out by the onslaught of costumes, never-ending doorbells, and the allure of the hazardous chocolate. There are a few things that owners can do to allow their dogs to have an easier time on Halloween, and be sure that trick-or-treaters are not threatened, or worse, by an overly stressed out dog.

☆ Teaching your dog that the doorbell is something that does not require him to go charging can be a fun game.

» Have someone ring your doorbell while you have some treats at the ready and as soon as the doorbell makes a sound, drop the treats in front of the dog. Do this exercise close to the door because that is where the dog will want to be. Repeat this exercise every time the doorbell rings, and once your dog is happily looking at you when the doorbell rings and not charging the door, it is time to move this away from the door a foot or two and begin again.

Each time the distance from the door increases, your dog will want to move back to the door or his last position. But because you will drop the treats in front of your dog and have only increased the distance a little from your last location, he should choose the treats over the door. (If he doesn't, you have increased the distance too much, so reduce and begin again.) Every time you increase the distance, it will be like teaching this exercise for the first time. When he looks at you without running to the door when the doorbell rings, in each new position away from the door, it is time to increase the distance again. Do this until you are completely out of sight of the door and your dog looks at you when the doorbell rings without running to the door.

Doorbell games are also a good time to have a Manners Minder in another room, with you hitting the button to remotely deliver the treats whenever there is someone at the door.

☆ Your dog might also be happier spending Halloween in a room far from the door with a great puzzle toy like a Kong or Twist 'n Treat to keep her occupied.

☆ Some dogs will need a calming supplement or even medication if they are really stressed out—talk to your veterinarian about this option.

☆ Playing calming music produced specifically for dogs throughout the night could help. Through a Dog's Ear makes relaxing CDs and downloads for a variety of situations.

☆ Be sure the candy dish for your trick-or-treaters is well out of your dog's reach. Chocolate is highly toxic for dogs and can be fatal, depending on the amount they ingest.

☆ Once your kids have come home with their goodies, be sure to store all their candy well out of your dog's reach.

CHAPTER FOURTEEN

Words for Christmas?

By Indy's fifteenth-month assessment by the Child Find Nurse, there was some concern that he was not building a foundation for communicating. He was not following a pointer or indicator, not following simple requests, had no words (not even "mama" or "dada"), and was not interacting with us in directed play—a back-and-forth play that would have us each playing a portion of a game.

It didn't surprise me that, like so many of us in our house, Indy was lacking in some areas and yet excelled in others. He was clearly mechanically inclined, given his talent for dismantling his Pack 'n Play, and he was quite social and even a flirt when in public. But with no words at all and no apparent interest in communicating needs or desires, he was given another assessment and enrolled in New York State's Early Intervention Program.

Probably typical of other parents in this situation, Lawrence and I were on opposite sides in our feelings about this. I looked at it as an opportunity to better prepare Indy for his education and life in general. Lawrence's early struggle with stuttering left him sensitive to these types of issues. It took him time to accept that, although there was no doubt Indy was a great problem solver and a social child who was always making connections that surprised us, he needed some help to start talking and communicating. I reminded Lawrence that both of us could have benefited from some early assistance, me for my dyslexia and Lawrence for his stuttering.

There were two ironies in this situation that were not lost on me. The first was that the most profound work Boo ever did as a therapy dog was bringing voice to a six-year-old boy who had not spoken a word before meeting Boo. I wondered why Boo's magic wasn't working with Indy, but had to remind myself that Indy was only fifteen months old and we would get there. The second irony was that my work with Pinball, and so many other dogs, was all about communication. Once dogs can understand what we want and we can understand what they want and can do, training is much easier. It seems like magic to the outside observer, but it is simply learning a mutual language.

There is not a person who knows me who doesn't know that I see the world through dog-training vision. I can relate almost everything, from international politics to baby care, in dog-training terms and while I know it makes perfect sense to me, sometimes I wonder if I am overreaching in my comparisons.

Our assigned special education teacher, Rona, was working on her applied behavioral analysis (ABA) degree. She was excited to be working with a dog trainer because so much of the research in the world of behavioral analysis is done with non-human animals, many of them dogs. When we started working, she explained to me, with some apology in her voice, that we would be using food as a reinforcer for the behaviors we would be teaching Indy. I was thrilled and giggled a bit out of relief, even offering my extra bait bag if necessary. She went on to clarify that a lot of her work would be observation at first and then it would look like play. This thrilled me, too. I find my clients often want me to come into a dog behavioral consultation and wave a magic wand that fixes everything right away. Or they want me to have some magic word or gesture that makes the dog stop misbehaving, when in fact I have to observe the dog and, when training does begin, it is usually best for the dog (and the human) when it resembles play.

Lawrence was still a stay-at-home dad, so for the first few months both he and I were involved in the sessions so we could re-create the exercises Rona was introducing for Indy at home as best as possible. We began with directed play so we could establish a basis for communication by taking turns. It went like this: I said, "Mommy's turn," and then I stacked some blocks and said, "Indy's turn," and then he stacked some blocks. From this simple exchange, we were able to start to do some basic communication and skill building that I still use today when I need Indy to help me put away all his puzzle pieces scattered across the living room. We then moved on to silly games that Indy loved, such as roaring like a lion on command, or putting a block on his head to build imitation skills. Although it might sound silly, it allowed all of us to have fun while we built his ability to follow directions, learn to imitate, and begin the back and forth that creates communication.

For me, this instruction was just like the tricks class I was teaching at the time. With Indy we were slowly building very complicated skills, and in class we were building tricks for the dogs. In both situations, we started with our criteria very low and increased the difficulty little by little. I joked in class that I was also clicker-training my son and everyone laughed, not realizing how serious I was.

Rona and I had many detailed conversations on the Premack Principle, the function of behavior, and other topics that would bore the pants off most people. But for Lawrence and me, it was just what we needed to embrace this process and to let Lawrence accept that this intervention was not the old school of labels and ridicule that he and I had faced. It also helped me to demystify for Lawrence the exercises I needed him to do with Pinball. For Pinball's resource guarding and integration with Indy, we were doing the same lowering of the criteria so we could build it up to our ultimate goal. Lawrence was no longer trapped in the notion that Pinball should do what we told him to, just because. Instead, he was starting to realize that Pinball, like Indy, was slowly building better and better behaviors.

With a little more relaxed atmosphere surrounding Pinball's issues, he was rebounding from the backslide that had occurred after our trip. He was back to releasing everything we asked him to—eventually, but without the whale eye warning, so it had to be considered successful progress. He was still helping me out with two extremely shy clients twice a month and loved his work. Pinball works well with shy dogs to help them build confidence. It is as if he reads them, adjusts his play, and then sort of says to them in dog, "Come on, it will be fun. Give it a try." Every time he has worked on a shy dog case with me, he has been a huge factor in transitioning the client's dog. His interactions with the human clients have also been good. Much to my chagrin, he still jumps, albeit gently, but then after being reminded not to jump, snuggles up against the person and squeaks a happy whinny squeak as he gets petted. Every one of my clients who have worked with Pinball have at some point expressed their love for him. It is hard to look at Pinball when he is doing such good work and remember just how bad he can be when he is afraid or pushed to the brink. He is an ongoing reminder that dogs, like so many humans, are not all black and white. We all have strengths and weaknesses that make up the whole of who we are.

Santa did not bring the gift of speech to Indy for his second Christmas, but we did have another milestone in the household. There was such good progress with the dogs that all three of them got to come share in our holiday get-together with Jill, Linda, and Teddi—no management, no gates, just fun. Porthos was overly exhausted by the visit, but I hoped it was just the wear and tear of his various conditions. Boo was starting to show his age, stumbling more and recovering more slowly when he bumped into things. But even so, he tried to work the room in his usual Boo-style (not unlike a candidate working a fundraiser). I realized I had to start thinking about retiring him completely from all his visiting in the New Year. Pinball was the perfect gentle dog as he went from person to person greeting happily, with only a small hint of worry. In the past he had been wary around some guests, but for this get-together he was happy and interested. That was a gift.

Winter set in early that year and by the middle of December, we had enough snow that I had to start cancelling classes and private sessions due to weather. Luckily, Lawrence had spent the summer chopping wood so we would have enough to keep warm and snuggled through April. Just as we managed the dogs, we managed the open roaring fire with a fireplace gate that kept Indy at least three feet from the hearth. Lawrence, Indy, and I had a quiet Christmas with the dogs and Freya, and then Indy went to spend New Year's with his grandparents. This arrangement allowed us to completely eliminate the question of what to do with Pinball for their holiday visit. Their relationship with Pinball had still not been repaired and I didn't know if it ever would be.

• • •

Training Tips You Can Try at Home

★ Clicker Training
★ The Premack Principle
★ Function of Behavior

Clicker Training, the Premack Principle, and Function of Behavior are three important behavioral and training principles. I am only offering general outlines and applications for these three concepts and how they apply in a household with dog and child. Googling any of these will uncover a host of details.

★ **Clicker Training** is a useful shaping tool for many types of training. The clicker is a small device that is used as a marker for a desired behavior. We can use a verbal "yes" or "good," but the clicker is much more precise. I like to use clickers when training specific tricks that require very precise markers in order to achieve the final goal.

We start by having a final goal in mind and then click and reward all behaviors that are moving in the direction of our final goal. We might chain backward as I did in the fetch example, or we might train from the first step as I did when teaching Pinball to ride a skateboard. First, I clicked him for sniffing the skateboard, then clicked him for putting his paw on the skateboard, and then clicked him for moving when his paw was on the skateboard. Although I didn't use a clicker for his resource guarding, it was a similar process in that I started with a goal in mind, worked with the behavior I could achieve initially, and then improved the behavior little by little. With Indy we used the same techniques to move him from no sounds to making an "Mmmm" sound for milk, then a "Pa" sound for his pegs, and so on.

☆ I don't usually recommend using a clicker when there are small children around. Not because of dangers, but because there are already so many things that parents have to be doing all at once that the addition of one more thing to hold and keep track of is often too much. If, however, you are already using a clicker, you can continue to use it to mark your dog's good behavior around your child.

☆ The other complication with clickers and kids is that small children think the clicker is nifty and they want to play with it, clicking it randomly and all over the house. This blows the power of the clicker or just plain confuses the dog. Either way, it will make the click meaningless to the dog. So if you are already using a clicker to mark good behaviors, please be sure it does not fall into the hands of your kids.

★ **The Premack Principle** was developed by Dr. David Premack, a professor emeritus of psychology at the University of Pennsylvania, who started his career in primate research in 1954. He is one of the few people in this world whose name can be used as a verb. To Premack something in dog-training terms means to use a behavior the dog wants to do in order to reinforce a behavior the dog is less likely to want to do. If your dog likes to go outside, then you ask your dog to *sit* before you let her outside. The act of going outside reinforces the *sit*. The version of this theory we use with kids is, "Eat your veggies and you can have dessert."

It is a little more complicated than that because the emotion of anticipation is powerful and often greater than the satisfaction of actually having something. When we Premack something, we are turning the behavior the dog didn't want to do into an enjoyable behavior because she is anticipating the rewarding behavior as she is doing the first behavior.

For example, if I hated dusting but loved chocolate I might Premack myself to always dust before I have some chocolate. In the short term I would get my dusting done with a reward, but in the long term I might actually begin to love dusting as much as I love chocolate.

☆ We can also use the Premack Principle when we are setting up the relationship between our child and our dog. If they both love going outside for walks, we can set them down together—the dog in a *settle* and the child sitting close by with a book. We can read to the child or the child, if old enough, can read to the dog. Throughout this exercise, we are guiding the child in how to appropriately pet the dog because most kids will want to reach out to touch the dog as they are reading. The petting reinforces the reading, and the whole interaction is reinforced when the reading session is complete and they both get to go out for their walk. They both get reinforced for quiet interaction by the walk, and both the reading and the walking become positive relationship-building events for the child and the dog.

★ Function of Behavior applies to understanding all behaviors—dogs, kids, adults, nation states. It refers to understanding why a behavior is occurring. It is not enough just to say that the child is acting out, nor is it enough just to say the dog is barking. We have to ask, "What function does that behavior serve?" Is the dog barking because he wants attention? Because there is something outside that is scaring him or just putting him on alert? Stopping the barking would require a different answer in each case.

☆ When a dog growls at a child, what is the function of that growl? Often no one asks that question and the dog is punished. If we don't understand the function of that behavior, we run a big risk of making things worse. Generally, the growl functions as the dog's request for a scary thing to stop or go away.

☆ When a dog barks at a child, what is the function of that bark? Once again, this question is often not asked and the dog is just told to be quiet. Sometimes that works and sometimes it does not. This mixed result is probably because dogs bark for many different reasons:

» Attention barking: "Pet me," "Play with me," or "I have to go out" are just a few. This dog wants attention and if you give him attention, the barking will stop for the moment, but he will repeat the demand barking more often and with more insistence because it was rewarded/reinforced by the attention we gave him.

» Alert or warning: "Hey, there goes a squirrel," or "Stranger in the house," or "That kid is walking funny and coming straight at me—someone please stop him" are some examples of alert barking. This dog needs to be redirected or moved away from the trigger she is barking at. She will also probably increase barking over time if we just yell at her to stop.

» Uncontrolled excitement or joy: This is the dog who is overjoyed to see you or overjoyed at something. Like Dante

TRAINING TIPS

walking along the beach, ears in the breeze, barking as if he was singing a happy tune. This dog will generally extinguish this bark within a reasonable time and we often think it is because we have told him to stop—but in reality dogs usually don't do this one for very long.

☆ If you want your dog to stop doing something you don't like, it is important to understand the function of what she is doing so you can tailor a replacement behavior for the dog or alleviate the stress causing the behavior.

CHAPTER FIFTEEN

When to Add, Train, or Rehome a Dog

....

I have never given up a dog, and hope to never feel the need to. The universe does not give us the dogs we want, but the dogs we need or who need us. These two personal refrains have never been so profoundly, and terrifyingly, challenged as with Pinball.

It is one thing to council a family with a small child and a dog with issues, but it is quite another thing to be that family. Pinball was a poster-puppy for the type of dog who probably would not remain in most homes with small children. My choice to keep him with us was, no doubt, controversial and was not necessarily a recommendation for others. My decision was based on my attachment to him and my need to follow through with my promises—whether to a dog or a person.

There were days I asked myself if the dogs were happy with the new configuration of our family; conversely, I wondered if Indy would grow up fond of the dogs or resentful of them. Would Pinball one day, in an irrational fit of fear or over-exuberance, knock Indy over or bite him? Would Porthos have one of his seizures and unintentionally injure Indy? Would Indy witness one of Porthos's seizures and be traumatized by the episode? Could clumsy Boo—bumping into furniture, walls, and us—one day knock Indy over and hurt him? All of these were possible, but it was also possible that they would never happen. My hope was that with an awareness of what could happen, Lawrence and I would be ready to prevent it through training, management, and guidance.

When deciding whether to train their dogs, most people want to know if they need a trainer. Many parents will say, "I've had dogs before and we have a good dog, so why would we spend money on a trainer?" Sometimes it is not necessary, but a good trainer will always be helpful, if only to offer an outside perspective. However, as soon as something becomes an issue (the dog growls or barks at the baby, or the dog avoids the baby, or even something minor such as the dog's potty training becomes unreliable when the baby arrives), it is time to call a professional trainer. Other questions families have—such as how and where to look for a trainer, what type of training to look for, and whether to choose classes or private training—are all addressed in this chapter and in Chapter Eight.

Parents often ask if kids can attend my classes. I like having kids in classes so I can teach them how to behave around dogs in order to help them avoid the statistically high risk of being bitten by their dogs, but I have to ask the parents if they think their children will be interested and attentive enough to participate in the class. I have had families of five in class with their dogs and some parents who preferred to come to class alone—almost as a mommy- or daddy-only event. The more I can involve kids in the training process, the better the dog's relationship will be with everyone.

The majority of the calls I get for training dogs with kids occur when a family brings a new puppy or adult dog into a home with children. Although I also get calls when a new baby is brought into a home with a dog who already lives there, this call is not as frequent. Often, when there are conflicts between a new baby and the dog, the dog loses because the time after a new baby comes home is filled with stress, sleeplessness, and (sometimes) financial limitations, and as a result the trainer is not called.

When to get a new dog or an additional dog is a tough decision for any family, and in my professional practice I rarely see a family with a child under the age of two getting a new dog. However, there are enough who do that many shelters and breeders have put policies in place preventing their dogs from being placed with a family who has children under three years old. Although there is no magic age when kids suddenly understand how to behave around dogs, the demands of caring for younger children often make it difficult or impossible for parents to appropriately introduce a new dog to very young children.

The ideal training setup for a family with younger kids and a new dog is a private session with all the members of the family, followed by a basic class. This training configuration allows you to jump-start the puppy's in-home skills and gives the trainer time to instruct the kids with the dog to achieve the best interactions for everyone. It also allows the family to get direction on handling typical puppy problems such as nipping, jumping, and potty training. The follow-up classroom training is typically the best bang for the family's buck, and a good way for them to train while socializing the new dog. However, some families cannot do classroom training because of multiple commitments and scheduling conflicts. In this case, private consultations are their only option. The cost of any training has to be included in the puppy-planning budget, along with the cost of annual veterinary visits, food, and flea and tick prevention.

Regardless of which option you choose, it is important that

your trainer understand what you need, given your household situation. Your trainer should have you fill out a questionnaire before a private consultation so he or she has an idea what your home is like and what issues prompted you to contact a trainer. This questionnaire will also help you solidify what you need to accomplish with your dog.

In the classroom, the best sign that you will get the flexibility you need is if the trainer offers individualized help as each student tries to execute the training exercises and can tweak solutions for each dog-handler team. Your trainer needs to understand that each dog has different strengths and weaknesses, as do their handlers.

In my early years of training Boo, when I was having great difficulty getting him to focus in classes, I was given only one suggestion to get his attention. I was told I wasn't doing it right or had to just "Not let him get away with it." This suggestion did not work and, in fact, made him pull away from me. I realized then that all dogs and their handlers make a unique team, and your team may not operate exactly the same way another team does. It is your dog trainer's job to think outside the box and solve problems creatively, considering all elements of the family.

The debate over private training versus classroom training comes up a lot. Rarely am I called in for a behavioral issue when the dogs have gone through what I call middle school–level training: a couple of classes that built enough mutual understanding that the handlers could ask the dog for what they needed and also understand what the dog needed. Once the handler and dog are working together to find a mutual connection so they can become a team, trust can be built in either a classroom or in private training. The one advantage classroom training has is the natural socialization that occurs because the dogs are exposed to other dogs and humans.

Sometimes, however, private consultations are the only way to address an issue. Dog-to-dog reactivity, separation-related distress, high levels of phobias, and aggression toward humans are a few of the bigger issues that require private consultations.

Sometimes families decide they cannot live with or fix their dog's issues and that there is a perfect home for their dog, just not theirs—a kind of doggie Shangri-La. The reality of rescue is generally that the perfect match for a dog with issues is difficult to find, and becomes more difficult if that dog has a bite history or as he ages.

In one recent case I had both—an older biting dog. This family had two small boys, a three-year-old and an eighteen-month-old, and two rescue dogs, a ten-year-old named Sadie and a six-year-old named Bella. The family acquired both dogs before having children and had contacted the rescue organization, asking to return Bella. She had bitten a relative with whom she was staying during the mother's hospital stay to have the second baby, was barking at strangers, and had chased a neighbor's dog with some indication of aggression. The family was overwhelmed with fear that Bella would bite one of the kid's friends, but was confident that she was fine with their children.

Because of the conflicting nature of this report, the rescue asked me to assess the dog for rehoming. They were quite frank with me that at six years old, in her second home (she had already been rehomed previously), and with a bite history, Bella's chances for another home were extraordinarily slim. While meeting with the family, I could see the tears welling up in the mother's eyes as she talked about rehoming her dog. It was clear the dynamics of this home would have been shattered if they had to rehome Bella. She was a huge source of confidence for Sadie, a source of support for the mother, and indeed good with the little boys. I was concerned that removing Bella would put Sadie in a position

I didn't feel she could handle vis-à-vis strangers and the pressure of the kids. I watched Bella play the role of buffer between the kids and Sadie, as she made a lovely split between Sadie and the older boy when he was headed for Sadie, easily and happily redirecting the little boy's attention to herself. It was also clear that Bella was attached to her family and the whole family attached to her. Rehoming her at six years old would not be easy on her or her family, and it would probably increase her fear reactions to strangers as she struggled to make the huge life shift that comes with rehoming. I offered to work with the family, and the rescue organization agreed the best bet for Bella would be to find a way to keep her in her home. The cost of a little up-training would be much cheaper for the rescue than kenneling or fostering her if she returned to them.

We worked on a couple of reactivity issues Bella had when out on walks, and we set up some strategic management strategies so the dogs could be contained whenever kids and parents were over for play dates. I reassured the family that it was okay to have their dogs hang out in another room for these play dates—this assurance relieved them tremendously. In the end, with some training and management strategies, we were able to keep Bella with the family she loved and allow the family to keep both the dogs they loved.

We got lucky with Bella because she was good with her own kids and could be managed when other kids and guests came over. However, there are times when there is no way to make the situation work. Sometimes, the dog is too profoundly triggered by the kids and the level of management required to keep everyone safe would be constant isolation for the dog. And sometimes, the parents don't have the ability or desire to work on the training necessary. There is no getting around the fact that training can be time-consuming and require another level of commitment in an already crowded life with baby and dogs. It is a choice that only the individual parent can make.

When these elements conspire to make keeping a dog overwhelming or impossible, the best option is rehoming the dog with friends or family members. But because that is not always available, the next steps are to contact the breeder or the original rescue organization. They sometimes have agreements to take back any dog they place. The last option for rehoming is offering the dog on the numerous online pet lists, putting up postings in veterinarian offices or on pet store bulletin boards, and advertising in local papers. Rehoming like this can be expensive and time-consuming because of all the emails, phone calls, and research into the potential adopter's references that are necessary.

The last and, for most folks, least desirable option is euthanasia. If we look at and accept dogs for what they are, we can usually avoid having to make the euthanasia choice by implementing training, management, and guidance before something goes wrong, and there are times it just doesn't work. Ultimately, no one can tell you when it is time to euthanize your pet, not for illness and not for behavior. It is a heavy personal decision to make no matter what the reason. I have counseled enough of my clients on this that I know the anguish this process causes, and when they have made this choice, I know they have had all the best information and have given their dogs the best assistance they could before making this choice. I have accompanied shelter dogs who could no longer live safely in the shelter at the end, knowing that the only solace I could give them was to be there physically supporting them and making sure their passing did not go unremarked. Folks can talk to trusted trainers, veterinarians, rescue groups, and even online discussion groups for advice, but in the end, only each individual has all the pieces to make this decision.

Training Tips You Can Try at Home

★ A new dog
★ Breeder, rescue, or shelter?
★ Rehoming a dog
★ Taking stock of the dog and kids before something goes wrong
★ What to do when the dog has lived with kids and suddenly growls at them?
★ When is it time to consider euthanasia?

★ **There are a number of reasons why you might want a new dog** in your family. Some straightforward guidelines will help you successfully integrate a new dog into your household.

☆ Timing is important.

» It may not be fun to have a new puppy that requires potty and household manners training when you have a young child who requires the same things. If, however, your circumstances demand this dual training, you can play one off the other. As the toddler is learning to pee and poop in the potty, you can explain to your child that the puppy also has to learn where and when to pee and poop. The puppy gets a reward for peeing and pooping outside, and your toddler can also get a reward for peeing and pooping in the big kid potty.

Probably the best reason to attempt this complicated dual potty training technique is that you have a limited amount of time when you will be home to train the puppy. The return to full-time work looming on the horizon, or an imminent deployment of one parent might make the dual puppy/

toddler training preferable because both parents can share the responsibilities. If there is not a compelling reason, then I would strongly encourage waiting until your baby is potty trained and has passed through his or her own puppy-like household destructive behaviors.

» If the new dog is an older, potty-trained dog, it is imperative to know with certainty that the dog is good with kids. Keep in mind that just because a dog is good with nine-year-olds doesn't mean he will be good with three-year-olds. Even with assurances that the dog is good with kids, high-level management strategies will need to be in place until you are positive this dog and your child have built a good relationship. Always keep in mind the Rule of Eight: no kids should be alone with a dog until they are eight years old. Many parents will fudge this number as they begin to see their children behaving responsibly around their dog and their dog behaving well around their kids, but it is a good starting point.

» A footnote on timing that is really only applicable for the northern climates: Getting puppies in the winter months will require you to stand in the freezing cold, sometimes in the middle of the night, to let your puppy pee and poop outside. For those of us in the north, getting spring or summer puppies is a blessing.

☆ The skills of the other dogs in the home must be solid.

If you are bringing a new dog into your home where another dog already lives, the new addition should only be acquired when the dog you have is where you want her to be behaviorally. In other words, if any of the dogs in your current household have behavioral issues or behaviors you don't like, don't bring a new dog home until those are taken care of, either fixed or managed. Dogs learn from other dogs more quickly than they do from us. Be sure the dogs you have will help you train the new dog and not undermine your training goals.

☆ You have the time to take care of a dog.

» I cannot even count the number of parents with new puppies who have said to me, "This is just like having a newborn." I, of course, said, "Having a newborn is just like having a puppy." It is important to ask yourself if there will be extra time throughout the day to deal with the demands of a new dog. Even though your child may be the right age and your current dogs may be in the right place, the crucial question is, are you ready to deal with all the puppy "stuff" like chewing, potty training, nipping, jumping, and exercise?

★ **Once all the items** above are checked "yes," then the questions are where and how. The question of breeder, rescue, or shelter is personal, but I can recommend research for all.

☆ Regardless of where you decide to get your dog, it is imperative that you and all the members of the household (humans and canines) meet the potential new dog before making a decision. If you have dogs and are bringing another one into your home, these dogs will need to live with each other on a level that even we dog professionals are just beginning to understand. Let them meet and be prepared to listen to what your dogs tell you. When we got Porthos, I had my eye on his little sister (the quest for a girl dog never ends), but she was completely disinterested in Boo and Dante. Porthos, however, came over and let Boo and Dante sniff him, sat and just hung out by us, and then cuddled in between my legs. They all told me who to take home.

Sometimes the suggestion of disease transmission is brought up, but if the litter has started their vaccination routine and you can show that your dogs are healthy and up-to-date on their vaccinations, it should be fine.

☆ Be sure to ask the breeder, rescue, or shelter if they will take dogs back if there are problems. Some will think you are referring to a refund, but I am talking about down the road, if something happens and you can no longer care for the dog. I often arrive at the Animal Rescue Foundation (ARF)—one of the shelters where I am lead trainer—and am told there is a new/old dog there, one who was originally adopted out but has been returned. Sometimes the dog has been returned because of circumstances (divorce, new rental housing that won't allow dogs, an illness that left the owner no longer able to provide for the dog) and sometimes because of behavioral issues.

☆ If at all possible, ask to meet the parents and siblings of the dog you are buying or adopting. This meeting is often easier to set up when dealing with a breeder, but sometimes rescues will have at least the mama dog there (usually waiting to be spayed) and some of the littermates. Meeting the parents and/or siblings of your prospective dog will give you some insight into how your dog will possibly mature. Even if you don't get a lot of predictive information from meeting the parents, you will get what I call the cut-and-run information. If a breeder has the parents onsite but says mom or dad isn't too friendly with kids and doesn't think your children should meet them, that is a big reason to cut and run and not adopt this puppy. It is not a certainty that puppies will have the same issues with kids as their parents do, but statistically the chances go up.

☆ Everything so far makes logical sense, but then there is the insurmountable hurdle of emotion. Porthos and Boo both rejected Pinball when I was fostering his litter. I reminded Lawrence that Pinball was going to be a difficult dog, but we overlooked all of the items I have listed above because of our emotions at the time. The result has been a lot of work. If you are committed to a puppy even when all the objective evidence suggests you should not be, prepare for the work ahead.

☆ Adhering to these suggestions doesn't guarantee everything will work out fine, but it will help you set yourself and your dog(s) up for success.

★ Rehoming a dog can be simple or one of the most difficult endeavors you have ever faced and everything in between. If your breeder, rescue, or shelter will take a dog back, that takes a lot of work and emotion out of the process. The other possible rehoming options are listed below:

☆ Friends, family, neighbors, and co-workers are sometimes good alternatives because you know them. However, statistically these dogs are likely to end up relinquished to a shelter down the road by their new family.

☆ Advertising can be tricky because there are a lot of nefarious reasons a person might be looking for a dog. So if you choose to advertise, it will be important to screen the potential adopter much as shelters, rescues, and breeders do. Have a form that folks can fill out so you get the information you need. Include questions like these: Have you owned a dog before? What happened to that dog? Who is your vet? Can I call your vet for a reference? Can you provide other references that I can call? Do you have a fenced yard? Will the dog be walked on leash? These questions give you good details and a chance to strike up conversations that offer even more information, like the buyer's neighborhood, work schedule, and so on.

☆ Shelter intake, too, can be difficult.

» If your local shelter does not euthanize for space, then it would appear to be a good place, but questions have to be asked. How will your dog do in a shelter? There is no getting around the fact that being in a shelter is stressful for all dogs—some do better than others and some completely meltdown. What kind of exercise and care do the dogs get at this shelter? Even though they don't euthanize for space, will they euthanize after a certain length of time? How do they handle illnesses or behavioral issues?

» Private rescue organizations and /or shelters usually have a limited number of dogs they can intake and typically have pretty strict behavioral rules. Most will not take a dog who has a bite history. Some will not take dogs who have shown aggression to anyone, including children, while some will accept a dog who has only growled at a child and then try to place the dog in an adult-only home.

☆ Sanctuaries are the Holy Grail of dog rescue. It is what everyone envisions when they think about giving up their dog—the proverbial farm where the dog can run free. However, they are hard to find and even harder to get a dog into. Occasionally, a rescue organization can get a dog into a sanctuary but it is even harder for an individual to secure a spot in a sanctuary, especially for a dog with a bite history.

TRAINING TIPS

★ **It is important for owners to take stock of their dog and their kids before something goes wrong** because of the difficulty in rehoming a dog with a bite history.

If you think you will not be able to live with a dog who bites, then rehoming should be considered if behavior starts to deteriorate and before any bites make it almost impossible to find a good home for your dog. Potential adopters should be apprised of the dog's issues and chosen to maximize your dog's success in his new home.

If there are issues—growling, avoidance behavior like moving away, looking away, or slinking away from the kids, barking at the kids, or other behaviors that indicate the dog is not happy around the kids—then training and management must be put into place even if you decide to rehome the dog. Because if something goes wrong while you are looking for that perfect home and the dog bites, the whole game is changed.

★ **What can parents do when their dog has lived with their kids for years and suddenly growls** at them one day? There are some steps that need to happen before the decision is made to rehome or euthanize the dog.

☆ Set up management immediately so you can keep the dog away from the kids unless you can be right there to watch the interactions and intervene if necessary.

☆ As soon as possible, make an appointment to see the veterinarian and begin making notes on your dog's habits of late so you can report them to the veterinarian. He or she will want to know about your dog's eating habits, water intake, energy levels, pooping, peeing, vomiting, and sleeping. Your vet will ask if the dog is allowed out on her own where she might have access to any wildlife excrement or urine, or be subject to tick bites and anything else that could cause illness.

☆ Begin researching and contacting local trainers, behavioral consultants, and behaviorists using the guidelines mentioned in Chapter Eight. Try these websites: www.avsab .org, www.aspca.org, www.ccpdt.org, www.iaabc.org.

☆ Try not to be overly encouraged or discouraged by the well-intentioned advice of friends, family, neighbors, or co-workers. The dog who has growled is not plotting world domination, but he will not just forget the episode either.

☆ Begin researching your rehoming options BEFORE a bite occurs, which you will be able to prevent because you have instituted step one—management.

★ When is it time to consider euthanasia? Unfortunately, that is a decision that has to be made individually. When clients ask me this question, the only answer I can give them is the likelihood of a behavior being fixed completely, fixed to the point that they can live with it, or not being fixable, and the level of work involved in these outcomes. My clients then have to decide if they can tolerate the potential outcomes and the level of work involved.

CHAPTER SIXTEEN

Whose Terrible Twos?

....

The terrible twos are a normal stage in a toddler's development characterized by mood changes, temper tantrums . . . The terrible twos typically occur when toddlers begin to struggle between their reliance on adults and their desire for independence.

While the terrible twos can be difficult for parents and caregivers . . . keep in mind that 2-year-olds are undergoing major motor, intellectual, social and emotional changes . . . However, most 2-year-olds still aren't able to move as swiftly as they'd like, clearly communicate their needs or control their feelings.

If your child is in the midst of the terrible twos, expect that you'll occasionally lose patience with each other. Try to stay calm, [and when] your child has a temper tantrum, offer comfort or ignore the behavior. Try to limit your use of the word "no." Instead, use other forms of discipline, such as redirection or humor. Also, consider avoiding challenging situations—such as [outings] during your child's naptime—and be sure to praise your child for appropriate behavior.

—Excerpt from Mayo Clinic online, by Jay L. Hoecker, MD

All of the above also apply directly to a puppy. Humor, patience, redirection, and limiting the use of the word "no" are all paramount in puppy training. I hoped my experiences with puppies made me ready for Indy's terrible twos. Although the ethology of the dog and human boy have some differences, they also have similarities when it comes to the things they like and the things that interest them, such as eating paper, chasing balls, eating worms, and generally carrying things around in their mouths. Many a bruise or bite/scratch has resulted from the early months of training a puppy for mouth control, and many a bruise—and in one instance a bloody eye—has resulted from a little boy who lashed out when frustrated. For a week after Indy had fallen and lashed out when I picked him up, Lawrence insisted I was a zombie with a blood-red eye.

The winter that followed Indy's second Christmas was one of the coldest and snowiest most of us could remember. Lawrence was at home full-time and my clients were limited because of the weather, leaving me at home a good chunk of the time, too. We all had cabin fever and not much relief from each other. Indy, while not yet in the terrible twos, was climbing the furniture to sit with Boo, learning to pet Boo and Porthos (who were both willing and interested in these interactions), and exploring locomotion over larger stretches of the house. Our dog walker, Karen, was still coming by every few weeks to spend time with the dogs, and they loved her.

On one of her visits the dogs were all together and happily playing when Porthos went for Pinball over a toy and Pinball fought back. Porthos was shocked that Pinball had gotten the better of him, and I was bitten while trying to break up the altercation. Porthos had not had an episode like that in a long time and I was worried. I thought maybe the cabin fever was to blame. But regardless of the reason, the hard-won freedoms that allowed the whole group to hang out together had to be dialed back. Luckily, Indy had been safely in the living room, well away from the dogs at the time. But Porthos and Pinball could no longer be together around Indy.

Porthos and Pinball alternated their time with Indy while Boo, as usual, was the go-between who was good with everybody. Porthos was removing himself more from activities, preferring to be upstairs alone than downstairs with us. He seemed to be in pain or at least some kind of discomfort when he was touched on the paws, and his water intake was way up with a frantic urgency. When a diabetic dog drinks excessively, it usually means his blood glucose is elevated and I thought perhaps his paw discomfort was possibly diabetic neuropathy. However, all the tests I could do at home were within normal range. I had four data points that told me there was something wrong with Porthos—the altercation, his isolating himself, his discomfort when being touched, and the increased water intake.

I took him in for a checkup and Julie ran a complete blood count (CBC) and a blood glucose test that was right on the money. There was no problem with his diabetes, but I had to wait a couple of days until Julie called with the CBC test results. Porthos had leukemia. While there was a treatment for this type of leukemia that could buy him a year or so, it included prednisone, which would make his diabetes impossible to manage. Given the reality that we could not treat the leukemia without making him worse on another level, nor could we alleviate his discomfort, which would only get worse, we euthanized him in April. He had lived seven of his ten years with twice-daily insulin injections, had multiple seizures along the way, suffered from chronic inflammatory bowel syndrome, and had obsessive-compulsive disorder that resulted in two major gastric surgeries. I couldn't demand he go through any more for me.

Porthos's passing was Indy's first loss and I wondered if he would notice. He did. In the months before Porthos died, Indy and I would stop by the master bedroom every morning to say hello to Porthos before going downstairs. The day after Porthos passed, I didn't stop in the master bedroom, hoping Indy would just go with the flow and head downstairs with me. But Indy insisted on looking for Porthos. Pointing to the corner where Porthos's pillow lay empty, Indy looked at me, his face a question mark without words. In a way it was a blessing that he couldn't yet ask me where the big black dog was. I answered the pointing with, "He's gone, buddy. I miss him, too."

After a long, dreary winter punctuated by the passing of Porthos, it was good to be able to get Indy out into the back-yard again. He loved being outside, playing either in his sandbox or his favorite game of carrying-the-empty-soda-bottles-from-the-recycling-bin-all-around-the-yard. I once again concluded that little boys and dogs have the same list of preprogrammed games when they are born because this was also one of Pinball's favorite games. Only he carried the bottles in his mouth all the time, which Indy only did occasionally. Indy and Pinball zoomed around the yard in the best configuration of dog and boy play I could imagine for them. Indy was still wearing his monkey safety harness attached to a leash I used to rein him in when he got too close to catching Pinball, but they were having a blast together.

At the end of May, Lawrence was offered a job on a Fri-day that started the following Monday. We had no idea how that was going to work. There was no way to get Indy into day care in two days, especially over a weekend. I had clients and classes scheduled for the next week that I couldn't cancel, but Lawrence couldn't really say no to a job offer. Indy took an impromptu trip to the Gramampies for the week while I collected all the records and filled out the forms to secure day care.

It was good to have Lawrence working and I was excited to get Indy into a school-like setting. Lessons about preventing separation anxiety in dogs helped me out when I dropped Indy off at day care for the first time. I set him down in his new classroom and as soon as he went to explore some of the toys, I said, "Bye, buddy," and ran out. I know from the outside it looked horrible, as if I were abandoning him, but I wanted him to have fun and not be feeding off any anxiety I had about leaving him for the first time. With multiple teachers and a small group of kids, it was the perfect place for him to settle in. And after the first week, I no longer ran out when dropping him off and could bid him a proper farewell with a kiss each morning. The teachers always remarked on how cute it was that after he puckered up for the kiss goodbye he happily ran off to play without looking back. One of the first instructions given to owners whose dogs are showing signs of separation anxiety is to not make a big deal about departures and arrivals so the dog doesn't feed off of any emotions related to those events. As I suspected, it works with kids, too—mine, anyway.

Day care was good for Indy. He ran in overjoyed each morning and was starting to verbalize much more, not exactly words, but many new sounds. I could see that kids in day care had the same advantages as puppies in play groups—good early social skills that prepare them for later social living.

Given how long dogs and humans have been developing side by side, it's not surprising we have so many parallels—from the games we play together to how we develop and our mutual, intense need for social interactions. There is no debate that the dog was the earliest domesticated animal, and the archeological record shows the dog as a separate animal from the wolf around 33,000 years ago, with the earliest recorded burial of a human with a dog around 10,000 to 12,000 years ago. Considering we include only that which is most important to us to our graves, that gravesite suggests how long dogs have been important to humans. Because of this long journey we have been on with our dogs, I have no doubt it has allowed both species to affect each other's development.

I thought of the many puppies I've watched start off as sweet, squishy love bugs, only to hit that five-and-a-half or six-month phase and become a pushy, don't-care-what-my-human-wants dog. I felt like those puppies had given me some readiness for the terrible twos that were in Indy's near future.

I was not surprised when Indy began giving me the look just after his second birthday. This look was filled with the words he didn't yet have. The look said, "No," or "I don't want to," or "Make me," and probably a few things that are not fit to print. Activities that had been easy before became a struggle. Diaper changing was now a kicking game. Getting him happily into his car seat was a challenge. He was in the ninetieth percentile for both height and weight, so I couldn't physically put him into the car seat and had been asking him to climb in on his own for several months. Now, however, he would either not climb in, or would get in but not sit, preferring to stretch out and play with the dome light above his head. At first I tried telling him he just had to do these things. And like every parent who has ever tried that approach with a toddler, I found out that was just crazy thinking on my part.

It was time to invest in books of stickers, a Pez dispenser, some fruity snacks, and Mini M&Ms. I started rewarding my son for the things I needed him to do. With Rona we had rewarded for specific foundation skills. Now it was everything. I would ask him to lie down on the changing table and let him pick the sticker he wanted while I changed his diaper—no gut kicking for me and a sticker for him, so it was a good trade. When I wanted him to get into the car, I showed him the sheet of stickers or fruity snack and said, "As soon as you are in the seat, you can have one." Voilà—he was in the seat in no time. After three months of day care, he realized he could play the I'm-going-the-other-way game in the parking lot. I laughed and said, "Your mama don't chase puppies; I ain't chasing you." I did the walk away maneuver a couple of times, and even though it worked, it took a lot of time before he finally gave in and came along. So I switched to a race—if he beat me to the vestibule, he got a fruity snack. He always knew what he was working for and he always got to make the decision to work for it or not.

The Pez dispenser was reserved for his allergy medication or days when he really didn't want to ride in his car seat. The Mini M&Ms were his super-high-value snack and mostly reserved for teeth brushing. It sounds strange to be giving a kid candy for brushing his teeth, but the alternative was a knock-down wrestling match. No more! He happily brushed his teeth or let me do it, and sometimes we forgot the M&Ms because we were having so much fun—we were fading the reinforcer already!

I know that this kind of parenting is sometimes viewed as bribing the child. But the definition of bribery from *Black's Law Dictionary* is "An illegal act where a person offers money or receives money from another person to influence the actions of a public officer or official." I prefer to think of Indy's rewards as business negotiations. I need something, he wants something, and we negotiate. Ultimately, I have two choices to get Indy to do what I need him to do: teach him that if he doesn't do what I ask, he will be punished, or teach him that doing what I ask of him will be rewarding. If I didn't have experience in rewarding dogs for good behavior, Indy and I would be at odds with each other and clashing over every little thing I needed him to do as he worked through the natural inclinations of toddlerhood—to challenge and test everything around him. If nothing else, I am preparing him for his working adult life in which everything will be a business negotiation.

There are times when I do employ the negative punishment quadrant of learning theory, too. For example, when Indy was banging on the sliding screen door in the living room and turned back at me with the look, which in this case said, "Whatcha gonna do about it?" I asked him if he wanted to be spending some time in his room by himself. He thought about my question for a second or two and then realized I would follow through on that suggestion, and picked something else to do. I know that these terrible twos would be all that their name suggests if I didn't have the tools that dog training has taught me. Indy learned there were consequences to his actions—good behavior will earn him stuff and unwanted behaviors will result in a loss of fun or stuff—and I have a negotiating tool.

The negative punishment also started working with the toss-everything-to-Pinball game. Whenever Indy engaged in this game, we moved Pinball to the back end of the house and the game was over. Indy was starting to learn that if he wanted his buddy to be on the other side of the gate, he could not toss him his toys. Unfortunately, the game was still pretty fun for Indy, so Pinball continued to have some toys flying his way. But at least Pinball learned that when something got tossed, he no longer had to fear it and either left it on command or happily took it to his pillow and put it down for us to remove it—for a reward. I was amazed at how far Pinball had come every time I reached down to pick up a toy and he was calm and relaxed. I did not, however, relinquish my management. He was still a dog with a bite history, and I still had a two-year-old son who was statistically the most likely target of any dog bite.

For all of Pinball's negative qualities, he is the one dog who has sat at my feet and snuggled up with me without exception through the writing of two books. There is no questioning his loyalty to or affection for me, or for Indy. Their relationship is growing into what I had hoped it would be. One evening, after I had given Indy guacamole with crackers, which he usually eats up like candy, he brought the cracker with guacamole to the gate where Pinball was waiting and slipped the cracker through the stiles. Pinball had a few soft licks of the cracker, and then Indy took it back and finished the rest. Although not thrilled with the exchange of canine germs, I was happy they were learning to share. Besides, Indy would have a great immune system if the canine germs didn't kill him first.

Indy could only spend time up on the chair with Boo if he was calm and sat without jumping because Boo couldn't tolerate much beyond that anymore. After twelve years of visiting kids and seniors, I officially retired him in April, just a week before Porthos died.

I am lucky that my friend Julie is also my veterinarian. She has always come out to the house to euthanize our dogs when their time has come. Each time, I let the remaining dogs see their fallen comrade, so they know what has happened. Boo had witnessed the passing of Atticus and Dante before Porthos, and it was clear when Boo walked up to Porthos's lifeless body that the wind had been knocked out of him. He had been Porthos's mama dog when Porthos was the baby of the family. After Porthos passed, Boo's decline worsened at what seemed to me to be an accelerated pace. By August, Boo had a fall. We will never know if he didn't know where he was on the edge of the couch or if he had a stroke, but he couldn't walk. I felt it was his time and called Julie. Luckily, she was not home and Boo seemed to walk it off, but not entirely.

About a month later, in September, Boo had another episode. He was unable to stand or lie down comfortably. Every time I tried to help him lie down or stand up, he screamed a blood-curdling scream. He refused to take any opioids for his pain, no matter what I wrapped them in. He wanted the tasty goo, but spat out the pill. I was left with nothing but baby aspirin for him, which could no longer relieve his pain. I gave him some valium to relax him and some melatonin to help him fall asleep. I knew as I gently massaged his ears, trying to help the medication relax him, watching his legs rigid and trembling with pain and discomfort, that I was keeping him here for us and not for him. I called Julie and we set up a time when she could come by, Lawrence could take the day off, and I had no clients.

Two days later, Boo lay on his chair in his usual spot after breakfast as Indy played in the living room with a new pizza puzzle toy that had dozens of pieces of pepperoni, mushrooms, and peppers. I was in the kitchen trying to occupy myself while Lawrence played with Indy. Out of the corner of my eye, I saw Indy standing next to Boo's chair and then heard it. "Boo," said Indy, clear as day, trying to feed the little wooden pepperonis to his buddy. For almost a year up to that point, Indy had been able to point to Boo and pictures of Boo if we asked him, "Where's Boo?" But he had never referred to him by name. Indy still wasn't referring to Lawrence or me directly, but for some reason, on this day he spoke to Boo. We knew with this final interaction, Boo had made his mark on the little boy he had waited so long to have in his life. His job was done; he could rest without pain for the first time in a long time.

Lawrence took Indy to day care and returned to wait for Julie to arrive. I didn't bring Pinball out to see Boo's body because when Porthos had passed, Pinball had been terrified. Instead, Pinball stayed upstairs until we got back from the crematorium. When I let him out after we got home, he sniffed all around the house but would not get close to Boo's chair. I knew he knew.

The next morning when Indy got up and came down for break-fast, he pointed to Boo's empty chair and asked, "Boo?" His look clearly said, "Where's Boo?" I can only hope the love these animals brought Indy will outweigh the pain of the loss.

Pinball was not taking Boo's passing well, so we started family outings to allow him some joy and some really great bonding time with Indy. They each wore their harnesses and leashes and they had a blast scrambling over rocks and through gullies, and investigating weird things on the ground. They played their usual games in the backyard, chasing each other with the empty soda bottles, Indy screaming in delight and Pinball smiling and darting with his tail waving high in the breeze until it was time to investigate mounds of dirt that could only interest a little boy and his dog. Then they both stopped and dug together. In the month after Boo passed, Indy's vocabulary blossomed and by the end of October he was naming things, asking for them, and eventually calling out to Pinball, but it came out as "Mimbaw."

Lawrence and I know that for whatever reason, Pinball is destined to be Indy's dog, and Indy has a special spot in Pinball's heart. I can only hope that I am able to control their interactions well enough until they have proven they are responsible around each other—not unlike letting teenagers drive with adults until they have proven they are ready to go it alone. I know Pinball and Indy will each make mistakes, which can be learning opportunities, and it is my job to make sure those mistakes are small and the lessons are easy ones. There are no guarantees for anything, but with training in place for Pinball and any future dogs, management strategies that are easy to implement, and guidance for Indy around the dogs, I can feel secure that we have given ourselves the chance to live a happy life with the people and animals we love. And in the process, we have given other families the guidance, hope, and wisdom to keep their dogs while keeping their baby safe.

It's All Worth It—
Dogs Are Good for You

My own experiences with Dante, Porthos, and Boo on their visits with children, seniors, and adults with developmental disabilities showed me how much positive impact a dog can have on all of us, particularly on children. Study after study has revealed psychological, physical, social, and just plain old *fun* benefits for anyone—especially children—living with dogs. I know as Porthos sat by Indy's side every night for story time and Indy reached out to let Porthos sniff his hand, there was a connection, a communication even. When we bring Indy down the stairs and hear him squealing in delight as Pinball runs alongside us, or Indy stumbles, looking back for Pinball, and giggles in anticipation of the furry blur that is about to go by, it is clear how much joy just watching that crazy dog brings into his life. When Indy would climb up on Boo's chair and hang out with him, or when he kept trying to give Boo some of his toys, there was no doubt that Indy saw all the dogs as his playmates and companions.

We have long known from studies that having pets in the

home contributes to children growing up with more empathy toward animals and more empathy in general. For me, that would be reason enough to have a pet. But we keep learning about more benefits that having dogs in our homes brings our children.

One example of these benefits comes from the research of James E. Gern, MD, a pediatrician at the University of Wisconsin–Madison, published in the *Journal of Allergy and Clinical Immunology*. Gern took blood samples of newborn babies and compared them to samples from the same children one year later. He found that children who lived in a home with dogs were less likely to have pet allergies—19 percent versus 33 percent. They also had higher levels of some vital immune system chemicals. Gern is quoted as saying, "Dogs are dirty animals, and this suggests that babies who have greater exposure to dirt and allergens have a stronger immune system." Although I cannot completely disagree with this statement, I would rephrase it a bit: dogs are not inherently dirty animals—they just *love* dirt and other gross things.

Other studies tell us kids who have a dog in the first year of life have 31 percent fewer respiratory tract infections and 44 percent fewer ear infections. Separately, Dr. Dennis Ownby, chief of the Medical College of Georgia Section of Allergy and Immunology, has found that when kids play with animals, the animals tend to lick them and this transfers gram-negative bacteria, which may be changing the way the child's immune system responds to help protect against allergies.

I had to laugh when I read these statistics because Pinball's fur is like Velcro and when he goes outside he returns with all manner of foliage in his tail and fringe. I look around the house and see leaves, twigs, ferns, acorns, and Pinball fur all around and I no longer become vexed at our inability to keep our home clean. I look on the bright side and tell myself Indy will have a much healthier immune system.

The caveat here is, of course, ticks, fleas, and other parasites. The overall rule should be that dirt and foliage are fine, but parasites are no good. Fleas, ticks, and other parasites are easy to prevent through the use of flea and tick products and medicine to prevent heartworm that usually has a broad spectrum anti-parasite element.

In addition to the psychosocial and health benefits of dogs, there are also educational benefits that children receive from having dogs in the home. When I brought Boo into the Stepping Stones classroom, I had no idea we would be seeing such remarkable results across the board. The results included one child speaking for the first time, a dramatic reduction in other children's ADHD-related outbursts that allowed for mainstreaming, an increase in the kids' general ability to focus in the classroom when Boo was there, and sustained focus for the weeks between visits as the kids wrote stories and made pictures for Boo. He was a major motivator in that classroom, and he is not alone. Teachers around the world, from the United States to Switzerland to Israel, have employed animals to help teach everything from responsibility and caretaking to reading and communication. Some studies indicate that children between the ages of five and eight who lived with pets attended nine more days of school during the year than those children who didn't live with pets.

There are some lovely ways to employ your own dog to help your children as they develop. The first one grows out of inviting your dog to hang out with you during story time. When your child is ready to read the book him- or herself, he or she can read it to the dog, who won't correct mistakes or be judgmental. Boo, Dante, and I did this reading regularly at library visits, and soon Indy will be reading to his own dog at home.

When potty training your child, it is helpful to ask where the dog or the cat pees and poops. Be careful, however, that your child does not take this question literally lest you have a toddler sharing the litter box or the backyard with the pets. I don't, however, think that type of mistake is unique to pets. A friend of mine's favorite quote from her daughter's potty training phase was, "No, honey, we don't pee in the salad spinner." There are plenty of ways kids can mix up where to pee, so why not illustrate that everyone pees and poops by letting them watch the animals—just keep the salad spinner up high.

Because of Pinball's severe resource guarding, I will be starting to teach Indy how to say, "Please," to Pinball when he has something Indy wants. Although this exercise will be a little tricky because I have already seen Pinball get more nervous when I ask him to drop something he has stolen while Indy is nearby, it should offer me the opportunity to illustrate polite sharing and cooperation to Indy. Even what we perceive as our most difficult challenge can be turned into a potential asset if we ask ourselves, what positive can I get out of this and how can I shape it to be better?

One of our successes from a negative was the Boo fortress-of-solitude. When Indy became strong enough to pull the pillows off the ottoman and climb up on the chair with Boo, I worried. Then I used this opportunity to teach Indy to sit politely with Boo. Indy was happy to comply, and I can only assume it was because he was so motivated to be up there with Boo.

Exercising, and enjoying all the health benefits that come with it, are easy when one has to walk a dog. As soon as Indy was coordinated enough to go out on the trail in our yard, Lawrence and I would leash him and Pinball up, and off we would go on an adventure in the woods. Dogs have a way of forcing us to be more active.

There is one mixed blessing that pets, especially dogs, bring to the table. Dogs and other pets can also be the domestic abuse canary in the coal mine. Mistreatment of a pet in a household can sound a warning that children and others in the home may be at risk for domestic violence. This information is something that schools and community organizations might be able to use to begin a dialogue that could potentially save families from abuse.

For some kids in abusive households, their pet is their only ally or confidant. This relationship can backfire, however, when family shelters won't take pets. Shelters for victims of domestic violence need to understand that often individuals at risk do not leave a dangerous situation because they cannot bring their pet. Allowing pets into these shelters or establishing an alternative space for the pets will increase the number of people who seek help, and in the long run hasten recovery for them on many levels.

It should be obvious that I love dogs. My goal in becoming a dog trainer was to help keep dogs in their homes and help alleviate any of the downsides to dog ownership because of behavioral issues. Those were also my goals in writing this book: to help families continue to love and keep their dogs, even after they have a new baby, by keeping everyone—dogs and kids of any age—safe and happy.

Notes

CHAPTER TWO

In April 2012, the Las Vegas Review-Journal *reported a story about Onion*
Lynnette Curtis, "Henderson Boy Celebrating First Birth-
    day Killed by Family Dog," *Las Vegas Review-Journal,* April
    28, 2012, http://www.reviewjournal.com/news/las-vegas/
    henderson-boy-celebrating-first-birthday-killed-family-dog.

CHAPTER THREE

Two-month-old Aiden McGrew
Andrew Knapp and Edward Fennell, "Infant Boy Killed When Mauled
    by Family Dog in Ridgeville as Father Slept," *The Post and Courier,*
    April 21, 2012, http://www.postandcourier.com/article/20120421/
    PC16/120429826.

CHAPTER FOUR

a six-year-old girl who was out playing alone with her family's friendly golden
    retriever
Vivian S. Toy, "Girl, 6, Is Strangled as Playful Dog Pulls Scarf on L.I.,"
    The New York Times, January 26, 2006, http://www.nytimes
    .com/2006/01/26/nyregion/26dog.html.

the chance of being killed by a dog is around 1 in 150,000
Robert Roy Britt, "The Odds of Dying," Live Science, January 6, 2005, http://www.livescience.com/3780-odds-dying.html.

CHAPTER FIVE
It was first named in 1936 by Dr. Hans Selye
Paul J. Rosch, "Han Selye: Birth of Stress," American Institute of Stress, http://www.stress.org/about/hans-selye-birth-of-stress/.

CHAPTER EIGHT
trainers who routinely use choke collars
American Veterinary Society of Animal Behavior, "How to Choose a Trainer Handout," http://avsabonline.org/uploads/position_state ments/How_to_Choose_a_Trainer_(AVSAB).pdf.

CHAPTER NINE
A tragic incident occurred in March 2013
Associated Press, "No Charges Expected in Fatal Wis. Pit Bull Attack," on WMTV Madison, March 17, 2013, http://www.nbc15 .com/home/headlines/Toddler-Attacked-By-Pit-Bulls-in-Walworth-Co-195688071.html.

CHAPTER TEN
Dr. Karen Overall specifically outlines the dangers of this drug
Karen L. Overall, MA, VMD, PhD, DACVB, CAAB, "Storm Phobias," *DVM360* magazine, September 1, 2004, http://veterinarynews.dvm360.com/ storm-phobias?id=&sk=&date=&%0A%09%09%09&pageID=3.

CHAPTER SIXTEEN
The terrible twos are a normal stage
Jay L. Hoecker, "I've Heard a Lot About the Terrible Twos. Why Are 2-Year-Olds So Difficult?" Mayo Clinic website, Infant and Toddler Health, March 9, 2013, http://www.mayoclinic.org/healthy-living/infant-and-toddler-health/expert-answers/terrible-twos/ faq-20058314.

About the Author

....

Lisa J. Edwards, CPDT-KA, CDBC, is the bestselling author of *A Dog Named Boo: The Underdog with a Heart of Gold*. She is also a Nationally Certified Professional Dog Trainer through the Certification Council for Professional Dog Trainers and a Certified Dog Behavior Consultant through the International Association of Animal Behavior Consultants, Inc.; a Pet Partners Certified Evaluator and Certified Instructor and an American Kennel Club Canine Good Citizen Evaluator. Lisa and three of her dogs have been registered active Pet Partners. Boo was a finalist for the Delta Society Beyond Limits Award before his bestselling book.

As a full-time professional dog trainer and behavioral consultant, Lisa splits her time between classroom instruction and private behavioral consults.

As a certified dog behavior consultant, Lisa is able to use her knowledge and understanding of the roots of behavioral problems and incorporate that as preventative exercises in her classes in an effort to keep behavioral problems from developing.

Lisa trains both animal and human teams for Animal

Assisted Therapy work and has been a regular Humane Educator in the Yorktown School and Mahopac School Districts. As the former Director of HART Programs, Inc., Lisa set up various Animal Assisted Therapy Programs in the Hudson Valley and New York City areas.

As a Pet Partners Certified Evaluator and Certified Instructor, Lisa teaches and evaluates teams for the rewarding work of Animal Assisted Therapy. As a registered Pet Partner with all three of her dogs, Lisa has done well over 300 visits with her pets, including hospitals, schools, nursing homes, group homes, residential care facilities for children with HIV, and crisis response at the Family Assistance Center post 9/11.

Acknowledgments

....

Three individuals were critical in helping me write this book, and I will forever be grateful for their input: my agent, Joy, for her commitment in understanding this topic's importance, and her patience with me and the process; my son, Indigo, for unwittingly volunteering to be at the center of this memoir and process; and my dog Pinball, without whom I could not have walked (with so many blisters) in the shoes of my clients and readers who have lived with a biting dog they loved.